DEVIL
IN THE DELTA

Photo By Rich Newman

About the Author

Rich Newman (Tennessee) has been investigating the paranormal for over ten years and is the founder of the group Paranormal Inc. He is also a filmmaker whose first feature film, a documentary called *Ghosts of War*, was released in 2010. His articles have appeared in *Haunted Times* and *Paranormal Underground*. Learn more about his investigations at http://www.paranormalincorporated.com.

To Write to the Author

If you wish to contact the author or would like more information about this book, please write to the author in care of Llewellyn Worldwide, and we will forward your request. Both the author and publisher appreciate hearing from you and learning of your enjoyment of this book and how it has helped you. Llewellyn Worldwide cannot guarantee that every letter written to the author can be answered, but all will be forwarded. Please write to:

Rich Newman
℅ Llewellyn Worldwide
2143 Wooddale Drive
Woodbury, MN 55125-2989

Please enclose a self-addressed stamped envelope for reply,
or $1.00 to cover costs. If outside the USA, enclose
an international postal reply coupon.

A Ghost Hunter's Most Terrifying Case ... to Date

DEVIL
IN THE DELTA

RICH NEWMAN

Llewellyn Publications
Woodbury, Minnesota

FIRST EDITION
First Printing, 2013

Book design by Bob Gaul
Cover art: House © iStockphoto.com/Shaun Lowe
            Cemetery © iStockphoto.com/Marilyn Nieves
            Lake © iStockphoto.com/tunart
Cover design by Gavin Dayton Duffy
Editing by Ed Day

Llewellyn Publications is a registered trademark of Llewellyn Worldwide Ltd.

Library of Congress Cataloging-in-Publication Data (Pending)
978-0-7387-3516-0

Llewellyn Publications
A Division of Llewellyn Worldwide Ltd.
2143 Wooddale Drive
Woodbury, MN 55125-2989
www.llewellyn.com

Printed in the United States of America

Contents

Prologue

I'm sitting in the dark master bedroom of the Martin home, waiting for something to happen. According to the owner of this residence, it was in this very room that the most dramatic of ghostly events took place.

After enduring several months of almost constant paranormal activity in the home (to include objects flying across several rooms, mysterious disembodied voices speaking from thin air, and unpleasant scents suddenly appearing), it had all come to a head one evening in this very bedroom—and ended with the family forever closing off the area. And now they did not venture into this space for fear of what might happen to them.

Looking around, I could see several more pragmatic reasons for not entering the bedroom; the entire floor was covered in a massive layer of dirty clothing, books, papers, junk, etc. Items that the owner claimed were strewn about by the "entities" that now resided there in the home with her family.

So now I'm perched on the remains of a bed frame straining to hear anything that might indicate something paranormal is about to occur. Joining me in this vigil are four members of a Mississippi ghost hunting group that I have worked with in the past. They had already spent one terrifying evening in the residence before giving me a call the day earlier. Wanting a second opinion concerning the strange happenings that were unfolding at this property, they had called me in to have a go at investigating the place for myself. And, having heard the tale that they told me about their experiences in the home, I immediately made the trip down into the Mississippi delta.

Once I arrived at the scene, though, it became apparent that there was more going on than a simple haunting. The woman of the house—I'll call her "Joanne Martin"— was, at first glance, the living definition of…well, let's say "eccentric." Decked out in a floral muumuu, she greeted us at the door with a toothless smile and a quick wave into what looked like ground zero of a massive explosion. As mentioned before, common household goods and clothes lay all about the double-wide trailer (Did I mention the residence was a trailer?), and a heavy blanket hung over the entryway of the now shunned master bedroom. If a ghost had done all this, I certainly dreaded running into it.

Now, sitting here in the dark of the night, I had to admit that there was a certain pall in the air—that feeling you get when you walk into a room just after a heated argument. Terri, a female investigator from the area, and I began rattling off a series of typical EVP (Electronic Voice Phenomena) questions as the rest of her team made their way through the property, attempting to obtain photographic and video evidence of the activity that is said to happen on a regular basis.

EVPs are thought to be the voices of the dead captured by audio recorders. Normally, these voices are not heard by the investigators when they are recorded live, but it's standard practice to ask questions anyway with the hope of getting something that will be heard later when the recordings are reviewed. We had been at it for about an hour and I was just suppressing a yawn when I asked aloud, "How long have you been here in this house?"

After a brief pause, a surprising—and alarming—sound echoed throughout the trailer. A sound that now sent the investigation spinning off into a brand new arena: one of sudden belief and possibility. A long, loud rumble tore through the bedroom, shaking the very walls around us. This was an event that Joanne had reported happening there in the past—and it usually preceded a whole string of paranormal activity that most would either label as being "poltergeist" in origin or a type of "demonic infestation."

I looked over at Terri who was now sitting in silence, eyes wide and peering into the darkness. "What was that?" I managed to get out…

Introduction

Since I was very young, I've been intrigued by the paranormal. I can remember watching reruns of *Kolchak: The Night Stalker* on television and keeping myself up at night to sneak into the family living room (without permission) to catch a glimpse of the occasional horror movie (*Trilogy of Terror* kept me up for almost a week, thanks to that little voodoo doll that hunted Karen Black in her apartment). And though I was into almost every type of monster or horror movie, there was something about a good ghost story that got into my blood.

When I was in my teens, my family moved into a circa 1920 house in Scott City, Missouri, that was pretty much on the verge of collapse from years of abuse by a former tenant. We didn't have much in the way of a household income, so we made do with what we had—and what we had was a strange, little house with hideaway/sliding doors, outdated plumbing, and an exterior that shed its paint like a cat in spring. But there was something else in that old house, too.

Apparently, we also had a very small and subtle haunting.

Every night, the old door to my bedroom closet would open all by itself. You could actually see the brass knob turn and hear the lock click as the door creaked open. Interestingly, the act didn't occur at the same time each night; I would invite friends over to check out the mysterious door, and we would keep a vigil over it for hours with no reward for all of our effort. Then, as soon as we tucked ourselves under the covers for the night, we'd hear the ominous groan of the door swinging wide open.

But nothing else ever happened. No apparitions, no disembodied voices, no cold spots, or anything else that we now typically associate with a haunted house. Just a door that liked to open by itself.

I took great pains to attempt to figure out the phenomena; no drafts came through the closet (though there was a small window in the closet for some reason)—and the door was not simply swollen shut because of a change of temperature and then opening when cool. There was also no suction occurring when either of the main doors leading to the bedroom were opened. Nothing seemed to explain the strange events. I would even double-check to make sure the door was completely closed tight each night (often multiple times), and yet it still opened!

So I know what you, the reader, are thinking at this point: did I ever try going *into* the closet and waiting for the door to open? The short answer: no, I did not. There were a couple of very good reasons for this.

First of all, I believed that this would in some way "invade" the space of whoever or whatever was opening the door (I assumed that he/she/it was actually living in the closet—or at least hanging out there frequently). This could upset the unspoken agreement that currently kept the ghost in the vicinity of the closet and that allowed me to sleep somewhat securely in my bedroom at night. This was a balance that I appreciated and would maintain at any cost.

The second reason for not waiting in the closet was that this would potentially be a terrifying event. Would an actual spirit show up in there with me? What would it look like? Would it be satisfied with simply opening a door now that a whole, live person was there inside the closet with it? And could I get out if something appeared? I mean, if it could open a door, it could possibly hold it closed, too, right?

These were questions that I had no intention of answering back then. I simply was not ready to directly confront such a potentially horrific thing. But the flames of paranormal intrigue were fanned once again. What are "ghosts" and how, exactly, do they come to be? I didn't know it at the time, but I was already taking my first steps toward becoming a paranormal researcher and investigator.

Years later, a couple of great new television programs would bring to light more information regarding the paranormal and hauntings directly to me on our old living room television set: *Unsolved Mysteries* and *Sightings*.

Watching paranormal investigators like Dr. Hans Holzer, Dr. William Roll, and Dr. Kerry Gaynor would fuel my desire to go beyond the spooky door in my room and explore other local urban legends, ghost stories, and haunted hot spots. Of course, I had no real idea of *how* to investigate a haunting, much less how to analyze anything I found at the site. So it seemed only natural that I would again turn to television programs to learn from the masters.

But back then, while watching the aforementioned experienced parapsychologists and investigators was cool, these shows rarely offered any *real* information on *how* to investigate the paranormal. Plus, the ghost hunting equipment of the day (analog audio recorders, film cameras, etc.) was much larger and cumbersome—not to mention expensive and hard to get (especially for a teenager with no real income).

As a result, my early "investigations" usually amounted to nothing more than me and a buddy going to a reputedly haunted place and roaming the area with a flashlight in hand. While such excursions were fun, they were almost always fruitless. But then, we were doomed from the get-go. Our ignorance of proper investigative techniques and tools of the trade hindered us from ever really experiencing (much less documenting) the paranormal—

though we did learn how to use our senses to monitor our surroundings (a skill that still serves me well today).

These days, however, information about ghosts and hauntings—as well as ghost hunting equipment—is readily available to everyone. With numerous books on ghost hunting, many television programs, and a wide availability of ghost hunting gear, anyone can learn the tools of the trade. But, interestingly, no book has ever really laid out the complications and challenges of working with individual families who believe they are suffering from a haunting—or worse yet, dealing with something altogether frightening within their home.

And such cases become even worse when the name of the "Devil" comes into play...

Dealing with your own religious views—as well as those of the family/client—can be the stickiest of wickets, and is not for everyone. These are the true issues and dilemmas that investigators face on every private case they take. Trust me, I know. Since my ghost hunting buddy from the old days, Mike Uelsmann, my brother Brandon Delrosa, and I created the group Paranormal Inc (www.paranormalincorporated.com), we have been involved with numerous cases (public and private) and know only too well the problems that can occur when religion and science clash.

Over the years, I have been frightened many times during an investigation. Sometimes this is simply the result of dealing with the unknown; at other times, it is because alarming events are taking place around me. But unlike my time spent in my old, haunted bedroom, I now eagerly go into the rooms with the ghosts. And it has been these trips into haunted places—and my experiences with dark and destructive spirits—that have guided my investigations. Which brings me to the Martin case and this book.

Never before has an investigation caused me more intrigue and frustration than this one. While reading this book, you will experience the same confusion I felt during my time in the Mississippi delta. It would take my years of experience, and more than the usual amount of patience, and an open mind to sift through all the paranormal incidents (and just plain strange events) that took place at this residence.

The "Devil" in the title of this book does have something to do with the obvious connotation of the word—but it also has as much to do with the old saying, "The Devil is in the details." Never has this been truer than in researching and investigating the paranormal—and the stories/cases discussed in this book are no exception.

Of course, when an investigator takes on a paranormal case, three things come into play: the past personal experiences of the investigator, lessons the investigator has learned at previous investigations, and (naturally) the circumstances surrounding the case currently being examined. And though I primarily use the Martin case to illustrate this point, I have also included past cases and personal experiences to give an overview of what I'm talking about when I say that personal experience and lessons learned can affect an investigation.

I have learned (usually the hard way) some strange lessons when it comes to investigating the paranormal. These lessons would ultimately help me navigate the new and strange waters of the Martin case—as well as allow me to see things happening there with a fresh perspective. After all, the Martins have only been around their own haunting; I have been around many of them!

Concerning the particular cases in this book, I have changed the names of those involved with the stories that are detailed here (except those involved with Paranormal Inc and where I've noted an exception to this rule) to protect the privacy of those involved, as well as the specific locations. And though these cases are the "stage" upon which this story unfolds, they are not the subject of the book. That distinction belongs to the aforementioned wicket: clients and their beliefs.

Have no doubts, though, that all the events mentioned in this book did, indeed, happen—usually with other people present to witness them—and that the included photographs were, indeed, taken within the locations mentioned (by me).

And what about you, the reader? Are you willing to go through the door and enter a place where something dark and terrible may lie in wait? If you are a paranormal investigator (or perhaps planning to be one) you will appreciate the twists and turns where this particularly beguiling investigation leads. But maybe you are like I used to be—maybe you just love a good ghost story and a good scare.

Either way, buckle up now and take a trip with me into the remote corners of the human mind, as well as into the dark regions of the Mississippi delta...

1

MY BACKGROUND

As I mentioned in the introduction, at one point I lived in a home with a mild haunting—more of a quirk, really, in retrospect. But long before that, I was born and raised in St. Louis, Missouri.

Though my family wasn't particularly religious in those days, my experience with God and the Devil was pretty much a sterile one: we would (on occasion) visit a grand church, listen to what the clergy had to say about the subject of the day, and then go about our daily routine with the threat of Hell hanging over our heads as a moral compass of sorts. For the most part, this system worked. It was straightforward, everyone knew right from wrong, and there was just enough fear to keep us from veering too far off the path of normalcy.

It was when I visited family in southern Missouri that I would experience…religion…of a more unique nature. My maternal grandparents were, for lack of a better church affiliation to attach them to, Pentecostal, and attending their congregational gatherings was always an unsettling event.

Whether it was people speaking in "tongues" or the preacher performing a faith healing on somebody (Why do they always have to slap them on the forehead?), something always baffled me. What were the snakes for? Why is that woman yelling gibberish in the middle of church? (I got in trouble for doing that.) But, perhaps, the most disturbing thing of all for a young person to digest was the idea of "deliverance."

For those who do not know what a deliverance is (and I'm not referring to the movie), think of it as a sort of poor man's exorcism. There are no grand rituals with priests in robes or chants in Latin. Oh, no. A deliverance usually involves a person flopping on the floor while other parishioners hold him or her down, with a lot of yelling and pleading (by the preacher and the afflicted), and numerous pleas for Satan to leave the possessed person alone. Then, miraculously, the person will suddenly stop fighting, stand up, and declare that he/she is now "free" of the Devil. It was never an extremely believable event from my point of view, but I certainly gave them points for showmanship.

At the time, what I didn't realize I was being taught, though, was that a deliverance held a certain, specific implication: that the Devil was actively involved in the everyday life of people and interacting with them in horrible ways. And while I may have had little to no faith that these preachers were actually banishing Satan from the allegedly inflicted, there was certainly some lingering fear that such a thing could be true—that the Devil could be all around us.

But even with all of these bizarre events, the most disturbing thing to me during my trips south was how these same so-called religious people acted away from their church. Whether it was the carefree, racially charged discussions around the dinner table or the general atmosphere of suppression and domination that seemed to exist in every household (especially toward women), nobody seemed particularly pious or holy to me. But, boy, they went to church, so all was well in the world, right?

Because of this hypocritical approach to life (not to mention religion), I quickly became jaded concerning churches and those who professed to be religious—and, as a result, the ideas of "Heaven" and "Hell" suddenly became ludicrous to me. Did we really need some make-believe place to reward and punish people? Wasn't that happening all the time right here on Earth? Besides, I always thought it was letting too many people off the hook too easy that they could "repent" about doing horrible things and then, in the blink of an eye, be absolved of all the wrongs they had done. How convenient for all the horrible people of this world.

Despite this bleak outlook concerning organized religion, though, my belief in God remained. To me, there is simply too much evidence of a higher power to dismiss such a thing. I mean, look around! And if anything is obvious in life, it is the fact that there are opposites for almost everything. So it seems perfectly logical to me that if we have "good" people on this planet, that we must also have "evil" people. And if we have God…well, there must be *something* on the other end of the spectrum. Call it the Devil, a demon, or whatever.

In addition to believing in God, I also developed a basic belief in the afterlife. This, too, has little to do with any church or religion. Basic experience—as well as the experiences of others I know and trust—dictate that such a thing is entirely likely. Besides, tales of seeing and hearing ghosts are prevalent all over the world. Literally thousands have reported experiencing them. And what are ghosts if not human souls lingering in some type of afterlife? This line of thinking has prompted me to spend much of my life seeking out haunted places.

Early Ghost Hunting

During my teen years, my family moved to a small town in southeast Missouri called Scott City. It was significantly more rural than St. Louis, but quite metropolitan compared to the area my grandparents lived—though that isn't saying much. And like most small towns, there are a lot of reputedly haunted places.

As is still the case today, often the biggest challenge involved with researching and performing a paranormal investigation involves figuring out what is *really* a haunting and what is simply urban legend. Today, computers and the Internet are a significant help. But back then, figuring out a true haunting was not so easy.

Some of the ghost stories that circulated the region were easily debunked with little more effort than spending some time at the location—such as the case of the notorious "Green Eyes" in Cape Girardeau.

This particular "spirit" is said to haunt the historic Lorimier Cemetery and is often witnessed as a pair of green eyes that's seen peering from behind a tombstone. Over the years, the place (in addition to supposedly being quite scary at night) evolved into a popular make-out spot for teenagers. Though I never made it to the cemetery in that regard, I did make a point of looking for old Green Eyes there. This (technically speaking) was one of the first investigations I ever did with one of my current investigative partners, Mike.

The two of us spent a long night tramping through the wet, dew-covered grass of the cemetery searching for the spirit to no avail. Then, from out of nowhere, there they were: two perfect glowing green eyes staring at us from the darkness. With flashlights in hand, we carefully crept toward the thing…until the eyes disappeared. Then, moments later, we saw them again. So we started toward the spot again…and they disappeared. This went on, over and over and over again.

To make a long story short, the eyes turned out to be nothing more than car headlights from a nearby street reflecting off a green marble tombstone. Quite disappointing actually. But it would be these types of stories and legends that would send me and my friends tramping through fields, rummaging through the ruins of old homes, and hanging out in abandoned buildings. And, other than the occasional cheap thrill, these places never provided any paranormal evidence of significance—with the exception of one trip.

A high school friend, Tim, and I were actually on a double date when we happened to drive through an area that had a reputedly haunted cabin. I say "cabin," but it was actually the remains of a small, wooden home. When I mentioned the haunted locale to everyone in the car, the girls squealed with delight and wanted to go see this sight. So we found ourselves, four teenagers, roaming the weeds and thickets surrounding an extremely unsafe structure in the middle of the night.

From looking through the cabin's windows, it was obvious that the floors had fallen through, so nobody went inside the place. Instead, we broke off into pairs and slowly circled the property looking and listening for anything that might indicate the presence of a ghost. Within minutes, boredom set in for everyone but me and conversation started to intrude on the ghost hunting (a situation that still happens to this day). Then I heard something. It sounded like low, male moans coming from inside the cabin.

I shushed everyone and called my date over. She strained to listen and soon heard the same sounds. Tim, along with his companion, circled to the other side of the house and quickly decided that they, too, heard a strange sound coming from within: a set of female wails. Now everyone was suddenly not quite so bored.

We would listen to the strange sounds for about an hour before leaving. As we drove back into town, we discussed the event. The final consensus was that we had either heard the sounds of spirits trapped in the cabin or that there was another couple there on a date somewhere we couldn't see—and they were doing better romantically than we were!

The strange cabin, though, was definitely an exception to what usually happened during my nights of legend tripping. And while these adventures may not have given me the ghostly experiences that I craved, these trips did manage to stoke the fires of my paranormal interest. Around this time, more and more documentary-style programs about ghosts were appearing on television, too. As a result, I began to learn more about ghost hunting and how to discern a true haunting from simple legends.

So it seems only natural that I would eventually get bored with life as a casual ghost hunting enthusiast and get involved with a more formal paranormal investigations group.

Paranormal Incorporated

After high school and college, life would intrude upon my desire to chase ghosts. It would be many years before I would discuss my intention to research the paranormal again with my original ghost hunting buddy Mike. It all began by looking at area ghost hunting groups in Austin,

Texas (my home at the time)—and, not finding investigators that seemed to have the same line of thinking as us (no psychics, no religious extremists, etc.)—I brought up the idea of us forming our own paranormal group. Like me, he was enthusiastic about the idea, though neither of us knew exactly how to approach such an undertaking.

In the end, I decided to co-create the group Paranormal Inc with Mike for several reasons: I was interested in the paranormal, I wanted some kind of confirmation of life after death, and I was bored. The undertaking of hunting ghosts seemed like a logical cure for all these afflictions.

Along with my brother Brandon (who joined with us a few years later when we relocated to the Memphis, Tennessee, area), Mike and I have since investigated many of the region's most well-known haunted locations. The three of us are pretty much the entire group, though we have no problem with working with other area paranormal organizations—and have, on occasion, teamed up with other investigators in large locations.

We approach an investigation with a scientific slant; if we can't capture and document an occurrence, it didn't happen. Personal experiences are great—they're the very things that motivate us to keep exploring the unknown—but in the end, if we do not get any evidence of the activity occurring, then we cannot support the theory of that location being haunted. Of course, that doesn't mean the place is *not* haunted. We have learned the hard way that ghosts don't perform on command and even the most active locations can go belly-up on you during an investigation.

Sticking with this scientific method of investigation, we also do not use any psychics. Though many investigators swear by them—and a select few individuals may actually have these abilities—there simply is no way to know what is truth and what is fabrication when a psychic provides information. To this date, I still have not found a single psychic willing to submit to a true challenge of their abilities. Not one. Until that happens and a psychic is proven to be authentic, Paranormal Inc will not be using them.

On the religious front, I am pretty much an agnostic. There is a built-in conflict of interest with organized religion/churches; mankind is supposed to avoid sin and the things that lead to sin, such as money and power, but these are the very things that most churches are founded upon.

I also cannot patronize an establishment that blatantly refuses to recognize facts that have been established by the scientific community—such as evolution and the creation of the universe. Until organized religions are able to reconcile their belief systems with science, I believe that more and more people will turn to other avenues to satisfy their spiritual needs (like investigating the paranormal). So, needless to say, we do not involve ourselves with anything of a religious nature during our investigations.

But, as I said earlier in this book, I grew up a Christian and attended a multitude of different church environments, and as a result, I still have a built-in fear of the Devil and

Hell. It angers me that it's there, but it is, indeed, there—good old Christian guilt and fear! At any rate, the point here is that my goals and methods concerning the paranormal are all scientific. This is an important fact to know as you read the details concerning the cases in this book.

Loving a Good Scare

As you've probably figured out by now, I have had a close association with ghosts and hauntings from a very young age, and I have always been interested in great, scary stories—especially those that are about ghosts. And since I have been hearing ghost stories since I was quite young, it's no wonder that I would turn to the paranormal for answers to life's biggest questions.

Whether it was my urban relatives in the north or my rural ancestors to the south, they all had one thing in common: they, too, all loved a good, scary story.

Many a night in my youth was spent huddled by the fireplace whispering tales about things like family curses, a "friend" who once was haunted, or even creatures who stalked the night. These hushed yarns were always purported to be "true" and they always happened to somebody that was personally known to everyone.

There were a lot of these stories, and many of them have stuck with me over the years. But two of these ghost stories have particularly had a large impact on me—and I credit them, as much as my own personal experiences, with pushing me into the field of paranormal research at an early age. Here they are as I know and remember them:

Ghost Story #1

This particular tale comes courtesy of my paternal grand-mother. It was related to me when she lived in Webster Groves, a small St. Louis neighborhood. Though the most well-known haunted home in this area was (and is) the infamous Henry Gehm house on Plant Avenue, my Grandma often spoke of another family close by that had their own unique and disturbing haunting.

According to the tale, there was a family living in this nearby house when it was broken into by a burglar. The man of the house, hearing the intruder entering the front door, grabbed a handgun and crept to the stairs from his second-floor bedroom. After peering into the darkness below and seeing nothing that would indicate an intruder was in the home, he started down the stairs. Of course, stairs creak and these were no exception, so the burglar heard the man coming for him.

So the intruder waited for the owner to get halfway down the stairs, and then he leapt from behind the living room couch and promptly shot the man dead. Screams echoed throughout the house as the other inhabitants heard the gun go off, driving the killer out into the night. I don't believe that my grandmother ever told me the out-come of the entire affair (Was the killer ever caught?), but I do recall the ghost story that followed the horrific event.

Apparently, the current (and altogether new) residents of this particular home were experiencing a recurring haunted event: each night, everyone in the home would hear the sounds of phantom gunshots, followed by the thuds of a body falling down the living room stairs, and ending with a series of piercing screams. Today, paranormal investigators term this type of ghostly event as a "residual" type of haunting—and most believe it doesn't always involve an actual ghost.

But back then, when I first heard the story, it was only one thing—scary! I mean, how could these people live in such a house? Weren't they afraid? According to my grandmother, they simply learned to ignore the ghastly sounds and, eventually, to sleep right through the nightly event.

All of this intrigued me. It sounded like something out of a late-night horror movie, yet I wanted to know more. I think this particular story has stuck with me over the years because it illustrates an important point when dealing with ghosts—there is more than one type of haunting. This was the first time I had heard of anything other than the stereotypical spirit, and it was intriguing to me that there could be multiple reasons to explain why a home is experiencing paranormal activity.

This would specifically come into play during my investigation of the Martin family…

Ghost Story #2

As I previously detailed, my mother's side of the family lived in rural southern Missouri. By this, I mean they lived out in the middle of nowhere—an area usually dubbed "the Boondocks" by Missourians. And I don't mind saying that visiting there was a dreaded affair, but not because of my family. It was entirely because of the quality of life they had and the living conditions on the farm. Going to Marston, Missouri, in the 1970s was like traveling back in time to the turn of the century.

A trip to my grandparents' house meant going to the bathroom in an outhouse, pitching in with the chores (these could, and did, often include chopping cotton, picking beans, and hauling hay), and, worst of all, constantly dodging tornadoes. A visit from a "twister" meant fleeing outside into the windy night and huddling in a damp and dark storm cellar that doubled as a storage area for homemade canned goods. We would all clutch blankets and peer at each other through the oily light of an old kerosene lamp as the numerous Bell jars of canned tomatoes and green beans clattered and clanged around us. We would sometimes endure hours of this until a storm had passed.

On top of all this, even the "fun" things in the country often involved work of some kind—such as slaving over an ice cream churn for an hour to get some dessert. Or trudging through the yard picking pecans for an entire morning to get a pie that would be hours away from getting into our mouths. This was just how things worked out there.

Of course, there was also, as previously mentioned, many a night of tale-telling. Nights spent at the hearth or on the front porch talking of dark things by moonlight.

It was during one of these visits to Marston that my mother, along with one of my uncles, told me a ghost story that I still remember to this day. Just down the gravel road from my grandparents' home was a neighbor who we would often see working outside in the yard. She was always by herself and seemed a lonely soul out there in the country all alone—but it hadn't always been that way. At one point, when my mother and her siblings were young, she lived with her son there in the old house. Her husband had died long before, so it was just the two of them there, eking out a meager existence.

Since they were neighbors, my grandparents felt bad for the widowed woman. As a result, my uncles would often spend the night at the house to socialize with the woman and to play with the boy. That is, they did so until the boy drowned just outside the house in a large drainage ditch. As you can imagine, this pushed the poor woman to the edge of her sanity. To attempt to alleviate her pain and loss—as well as to provide her with some much-needed company—my uncles would still, on occasion, spend the night with her in her home. It was during one of these visits that this story takes place...

My two uncles had finished playing for the night and the woman had just tucked them in for some sleep when they began hearing some strange sounds coming from the upstairs hallway, just outside the guest bedroom. These noises began as soft knocks and bangs, but soon escalated to the sounds of footsteps and even an unintelligible voice whispering from just outside the door. Needless to say, my uncles were quite frightened, though they did manage to eventually drift off to sleep. But later that same night, the two of them decided to make a trip to the bathroom together. (Hey, if you have to be pee and be scared, pee and be scared with company.)

According to them, while they were using the restroom, something kept turning off the bathroom light and knocking on the bathroom door. Once they had finished up, they immediately ran back to their beds and jumped under the covers. Eventually, they drifted off to sleep once again. But this wasn't the end of it.

Off and on, for the rest of the night, they would both feel something tugging at their blankets—and, on occasion, their feet. They would wake up, peer over the covers for any intruder, then, seeing nobody was in the room with them, they would dive back under the blankets. Much to their dismay, this went on till sunup. It was the following morning, though, that they received the biggest surprise of all...

After they had gotten dressed and went downstairs for breakfast, they heard and saw a strange sight: the woman of the house was going about cooking their meal—while having a conversation with nobody! When they asked who she was speaking to, she told them that her son was still there with her in the house and that she still liked to talk to him.

Then she calmly served them their food. I probably don't have to tell you that they never spent the night there again.

Years later I would see the old house, now empty, sitting there, falling into disrepair. Was the spirit of the boy still there? Was the poor, lonely woman (who was now dead, too) there with him? I didn't know, but I wished I could find out. Today that house is long gone or I would have certainly visited it. But it is because of these stories—and many others just like it—that I slowly migrated toward the paranormal. I was determined to find out how this whole afterlife thing worked. And if it meant that I had to visit every haunted place in the state of Missouri to do so, then so be it!

Another reason this story is important to me is that it illustrates an important fact for us investigators: hauntings happen to real people—people we often know and want to help. It's easy to forget sometimes that ghosts and hauntings are very real things that happen to unsuspecting families all the time. They are not just fodder for horror stories. The compassion I felt for that poor woman and her dead son—as well as the questions her story raised—affects me and my investigations to this day.

Performing an Investigation

Before jumping into the particulars of the Martin case, it's important that you know how I perform an investigation. In general, paranormal groups fall under three categories: Sci (scientific-based groups), Psi (psychic-based groups), and Religious. As mentioned above, I would definitely consider myself a scientific investigator. So when I approach a paranormal investigation, with or without Paranormal Inc, there are several guidelines that I follow:

1. Silence is golden. We try to keep our group very small (two to three people if possible) and we maintain noise discipline to keep from contaminating evidence.

2. Be a neutral investigator. I try not to have any preconceived notions about what is or is not happening at a haunted location. I have gone to too many "investigations" with other paranormal groups where the entire event was an exercise in sophistry. They were already completely sure the place was haunted, so every little knock, creak, etc., was "proof" of paranormal activity.

3. Be respectful of the location. I always try to leave a place in the condition I found it, and I always get permission to investigate. In addition, I feel there should always be some level of professionalism so that the client doesn't feel I'm just some thrill seeker who is there to see a ghost.

4. Evidence, not experience. Again, as I stated above, the goal of any investigation is to get audio, photographic, or video evidence of the haunting. This means I do not go into a room without equipment designed to do just that.

5. Detect, interact, capture, and escalate (DICE).
This is my basic philosophy for investigating.
First, I try to detect where the spirit(s) is by using
environmental monitoring gear (EMF detectors,
weather/temperature stations, etc.) and performing
a vigil. Once there is evidence of a presence, I try to
interact with the entity by performing simple EVP
work or asking the ghost to manipulate a trigger
object. All of this will be captured on audio and/
or video recorders. When it appears interaction is
happening, I then try to build on what's happening
by escalating the interaction, such as performing a
"table tipping" session or providing some ambient
energy for the spirit to attempt to materialize.

This is pretty much the foundation of all my investigations—and it has proven to be a good system for obtaining
quality evidence when a haunting is actually occurring. If
this method of ghost hunting appeals to you, you can always
read more about my methods in my book (shameless plug)
Ghost Hunting for Beginners from Llewellyn Publishing.

Believers vs. Nonbelievers

Interestingly, I have found over the years that almost
everyone is predisposed to believing one way or another concerning ghosts. For those who believe in spirits, almost everything constitutes evidence. The fuzziest of audio files are
voices speaking from beyond, common radios on "scan" can

tune in the dead, and Hasbro board games can allow users to speak to long-lost loved ones. (Yeah, you know the one).

On the flip side, those who simply think ghosts are hogwash cannot be swayed by any amount of evidence or eyewitness accounts. I have a good friend (an atheist) in Austin, Texas, who designs new technology for the scientific community. He doesn't believe in ghosts—and, most likely, never will.

When I tell him of being alone in a haunted location and actually hearing a disembodied voice speak right beside me, he says somebody is "faking it." It does no good to explain to him that I am alone, that there are no sounds coming in from outside, and that the owners are an elderly couple without the technological know-how to pull the wool over my eyes. Though he is a scientist, there is no level of scientific method that could be employed that will *ever* convince him that there are ghosts.

Furthermore, he loves to say "prove it" when I bring up the subject. I just have to smile. I know full well there is no proof that would ever be good enough for him— and, of course, he refuses to go along on an investigation. Why bother shaking up what he thinks of as "the truth" by chancing actually seeing or hearing something for himself? My usual comeback for skeptics is to point out that if they believe in science then they should believe what scientists say: Thomas Edison, Nikola Tesla, and even Albert Einstein have all indicated a belief in the human soul. Edison even claimed to know how to build a device to speak to the dead. So, how about that, Mr. Skeptic?

The whole belief vs. nonbelief thing also applies to religion. I have approached the owners of homes-turned-bed and breakfasts about performing an investigation on their property. It doesn't matter that the property has had a long-standing reputation for being haunted (often with some evidence to support it), if they do not believe in ghosts, or if they are members of certain denominations of hard-core Christian churches, they will not entertain even the idea of their home being haunted. To them, when you die you go to Heaven or you go to Hell. There is nothing else.

There is a well-known haunted inn in Virginia that was recently purchased by new owners. When I wrote them concerning a visit to investigate their resident spirit, I was told the only "spirit" there was that of "the Lord." What can you say to that?

For me, the question of belief was answered long ago. When you've been touched by invisible hands, heard disembodied voices speak around you, and seen a pale figure materialize in front of your very eyes, it's quite easy to believe. But we will talk about these adventures later…

What's important for us to know now (for dealing with the Martin case) is that cases almost always revolve around either a hard-core skeptic or a person who is already convinced he or she is haunted. Each type of person poses a unique set of challenges and accommodations and both types of client want some type of resolution to their haunting.

Haunted Locations

Despite the naysayers, there are a lot of haunted places. Don't think so? Just check out the first paranormal book I wrote, *The Ghost Hunter's Field Guide,* also available from Llewellyn Publishing (last plug, I promise). There are thousands of haunted hotels, restaurants, museums, B&Bs, and (most certainly) homes. Over the course of visiting many of these places, I have seen, heard, and been touched by ghosts. And it's always a unique and startling experience.

Because of this, for me the subject of the paranormal is not about, "Do ghosts exist?" It's about *proving* they exist and understanding *how and why* they exist. Famed investigator and reporter John Keel once wrote, "We must stop asking: Can these things be? And begin asking: Why are these things?" (*Operation Trojan Horse*, 1970). I agree.

It's interesting to note that for every place out there that chooses to capitalize on their haunting—or at least acknowledge that it's happening—there are probably a hundred that refuse to admit that they are experiencing some strange things. But, more and more, it is becoming quite accepted for places to admit that they experience paranormal events and to even advertise their ghosts. This is mostly due to a sudden surge in paranormal television programs.

For these haunted tourist sites, getting national exposure on a television show is the ultimate goal. And this has, mostly, worked in the paranormal community's favor. Ten years ago, if you wanted to do some investigating at a haunted hotel, you'd have to sneak around with your camera and audio recorder in the middle of the night. These days, you can approach the concierge and get most of the "hot spots" in the place pointed out for you. You just may have to leave a nice tip…

On the bad side of the television experience, though, it has released a whole new wave of inexperienced investigators into the world who are claiming to be experts.

Recreational vs. Professional Ghost Hunting

As I said before, it was a batch of television shows that sparked my original interest in exploring the paranormal, so I understand the concept of watching ghost hunters on television and wanting to do what they do. Unfortunately, though, television shows have producers—producers who want tension and suspense in their programs. Even when nothing is going on, they make sure the show is exciting. This is, of course, a concept that almost never translates to real paranormal investigations.

You can always tell when an investigator is a victim of these shows' high expectations; they fidget, they talk, and generally become bored long before an investigation is actually over. And they almost never produce any good evidence—even when they are at a great, haunted location. This is because they pollute all their audio and video footage by constantly talking, they give up too easily, and they don't take the time to properly review the data/footage they have collected (because this task is even more boring). In short, they are recreational ghost hunters. And there is nothing wrong with this—as long as they *know* they are recreational ghost hunters and do not attempt to do private cases.

When a researcher performs an investigation at a private home, the inhabitants will want answers! It's not like on a television program where you can do some sort of brief "show and tell" and scoot along your way. As you're going to find out while you are reading this book, investigating a private case means understanding the psychological elements of the household, the personal belief system of the family, and often helping them cope with what's going on in their house.

One of our investigators in Paranormal Inc was once approached by a coworker who claimed her home was haunted. She said activity was happening on a regular basis and that she wanted us to attempt to get "proof" so others would stop thinking she was crazy. It sounded simple enough. As we drove to investigate this location, I asked for more information about the case from my co-investigator. Where were the hot spots in the home? What kind of activity had been witnessed? Did the client have any idea of who may be haunting the place?

After thinking for a few minutes, he had to admit that he had none of these details. After talking about this for a few minutes, we quickly figured out that his coworker was being evasive concerning the details of her haunting.

She hadn't said who she thought was haunting the place or provided any details regarding the actual occurrences in the home.

When we arrived at the house and were taken on a tour of the premises, the woman (along with her husband) pointed out specific places where they claimed to have heard or seen something, but it was becoming painfully obvious that she was not telling us the whole story. So I asked her directly who was haunting their home. That was when she dropped the bomb.

Her teenage son had recently passed away on the property and she was convinced that he was there in the house with her. She told us this with tears appearing in her eyes. Behind her, her husband watched anxiously. I would later learn from him that she had been getting counseling from a psychiatrist since the boy's death. So, needless to say, there was more going on than us simply investigating whether or not the house was haunted. We could potentially undo years of psychological counseling and send this woman over the edge if we said to her that her dead child was haunting their home.

Conversely, it might even send her over the edge if we told her that he wasn't in the house with her! This kind of conundrum is common with private cases—and one of the pitfalls that cause a lot of amateur paranormal groups to prematurely make decisions about a case and, often, say things because they want to make the client feel better by saying what they want to hear.

We would go on to find nothing paranormal at this particular house (thank goodness). Seeing that she was a devout Catholic (statues of Mother Mary were all over the place), I told her that she should be content that her son was not there and that he had "moved on" to a better place. At this, though, she vehemently disagreed. "I want him here with me," she said. "I don't care if it's selfish." I stressed to the husband that he should probably make sure she still gets counseling and reiterated that the "haunting" of their home was simply wishful thinking on her part. He agreed and thanked us.

Imagine the scenario at this house if a self-professed psychic had pretended to speak to their dead son or if an amateur, thrill-seeking ghost hunter had walked around the house, jumping at every pop made by the water heater and claimed to hear/see something that wasn't there. Either would have been disastrous and might have caused irreparable psychological harm to this poor woman. Of course, there is also the possibility of another danger with this type of case as well…

Obsession

There is an age-old question that's popular with all ghost hunters: Why is it that some places are haunted and some are not? Having a death occur within the property seems to be no factor where this is concerned. Every hospital in the world has had deaths, yet you rarely hear of haunted, currently operational hospitals. Some places even claim to be haunted by someone who died in a whole different location—this is why there are multiple properties that claim the spirit of Abraham Lincoln.

What's the deciding factor that creates a haunting? Hand in hand with this conundrum is the fact that not everyone seems to see/hear ghosts. There have been many times over the years that I have visited a haunted place to learn that past residents had "no trouble" while living in the afflicted location. How can some people live for years in a seemingly haunted house without ever noticing a single strange event?

According to some researchers—and I have to admit that my own personal experience with cases seems to back this up—that the more a person pays attention to a spirit, the more activity seems to occur. It is one of the reasons that "interact" and "escalate" is part of my investigative method; the more you interact with a spirit, the more things happen. And, strangely enough, this can even happen in places that were not originally haunted! This concept is termed "obsession" by the paranormal community.

Because of this concept of spurring increased activity, certain clergy urge people to avoid communicating with any spirits they encounter. The presumption is that if you notice a spirit, and it notices you too, it will stick around. If we are to believe this concept, then even dwelling on the possibility of a place being haunted could (possibly) create such a haunted environment. And it has ...

A group in Canada called the Toronto Society for Psychical Research tested this theory in the 1970s by inventing a ghost named "Philip Aylesford" at a place that had no haunting whatsoever. After a few sessions of speaking to Philip, imagine their surprise when they started getting answers! Then, not only did the location begin to exhibit paranormal activity, but the spirit present seemingly adopted the persona of Philip. Since we know that there has never been a Philip Aylesford, who or what is speaking to these researchers?

If dwelling on the subject of ghosts can actually create a haunting, a whole new problem suddenly arises. What if the previously mentioned family had continued to speak to their dead son in their home? Would he have eventually appeared? Or would some random spirit be attracted to the attention and pretend to be their son? These are interesting—and disturbing—questions. And what do you do once the spirits are there?

When we examine the concept of obsession it's hard to not talk about the tragic case of journalist Joe Fisher. Most of what happened to Fisher was documented by himself in the book *Hungry Ghosts*—and it makes for a riveting, if not sad, read. The short version is that Fisher, while investigating a story about psychics who could channel the dead, became obsessed with a spirit that he believed was speaking to him through a medium that he trusted.

He soon became obsessed with this "spirit," who stated that she and Fisher were lovers in a past life. His obsession with this medium/entity became so strong that he lost most of his real-life relationships, including his marriage, and embarked on a quest to Europe to determine if the spirit was, indeed, a real person who once lived there. On this journey, he discovered that most of the information given to him were outright lies. Now, here is where Fisher's story goes terribly awry…

Instead of concluding that the medium provided false information and confronting her for lying to him, he determined that it was the spirit who was lying to him and that it was attempting to manipulate him for nefarious reasons. He left the spiritualist group and soon became paranoid that spirits were now trying to get him. On May 9, 2001, Joe Fisher committed suicide by leaping off a cliff at Elora Gorge, near Fergus, Ontario, Canada.

His death was a tragedy and left many questions unanswered. Why was he so convinced that spirits were after him? Were paranormal events really happening around him? Unfortunately, nobody but Fisher can truly know what was running through his head the day he passed away.

While this is an extreme example of obsession with the paranormal, there is still a lesson to be learned here: obsession is a very bad thing!

Ghostbusting

Blame it on the movie if you like, but there is a whole culture of paranormal investigators out there that believe they can "get rid" of ghosts. Some are even so bold as to post this on their websites. Huh? How can you guarantee to get rid of ghosts? And do we *want* to get rid of them? I'd hate to think that if I died and became trapped in a physical location, people would be trying to do away with me. I mean, where would I go exactly? Aren't things bad enough as it is?

Claiming to rid a location of ghosts is a bad practice. Besides the fact that there is no way to guarantee this, how do you *prove* a ghost is gone? It's hard enough to prove to some people that a ghost is there. These types of shenanigans are usually done to give clients a sense of relief—though this will be short-lived if the place is actually haunted.

So what can investigators do to assuage the fears of a haunted home owner? It seems a little cruel to investigate a private residence, show the client evidence that they are, indeed, haunted, and then to simply leave them wondering what's next. So what do you do? This is where the psychological and religious aspects of a household come into play. Notice I say "of a household"—not you!

At times, simply understanding the religious views of a family and suggesting an appropriate course of action is enough (you don't want to suggest a Protestant "clearing" of their home if they are a Catholic—this is a foreign concept to them). At other times, like the case I mentioned before, it's more appropriate to suggest a counselor or psychologist/psychiatrist. And, unfortunately, there are times when a family should simply consider moving if they continue to be uneasy with their environment. Moving is an especially important consideration if there are young children present who can be permanently scarred by living in an environment of fear.

Whatever happens, if you are a recreational ghost hunter, you should keep the contact information of a professional paranormal investigator that you can refer people to when needed. And if you are a professional, I suggest keeping business cards for a counselor and a clergyman on hand (I have found that Unitarians and Presbyterians are great for being open to blessing homes). The goal is to make the client comfortable in their home once again, and to find answers for them. This involves good counseling, research, and understanding who you are working for.

The Martin Case

Now that you understand where I stand as far as investigating private cases goes—and my opinions about the paranormal in general—be prepared to read as I continuously get baffled by the twists and turns of the Martin case and am often forced to reevaluate what I think of as "evidence" and as "paranormal." This particular case is also important in that it illustrates the difficulty that arises when we try to classify or pigeonhole a paranormal case as one type of event.

It was on a Friday when I received the phone call. There was a home that was under malicious, otherworldly assault in the heart of the Mississippi delta...and the owners believed it could be the Devil...

2

GETTING THE CALL

I could tell by the sound of Terri's voice that something extraordinary was happening in Mississippi. Though she belonged to a relatively new paranormal group, her band of investigators had explored some pretty heavily haunted locations. So when she said they needed assistance on a case that involved a haunted home, a young man who was suffering the occasional possession, and activity that was off the charts, I was most certainly intrigued.

According to the homeowner, Joanne Martin, her family had been experiencing paranormal activity on a regular basis since they had moved into a double-wide trailer on her family's land in 2000. They were accustomed to this, however, and had learned to simply live with the constant otherworldly attention. It was only during the last year that the activity had suddenly escalated to the point that she felt compelled to call upon paranormal researchers for assistance.

There were five individuals currently living in the Martin premises: Joanne, her daughters Julie and Katie, and a couple in their twenties who were renting a room from the Martin family (I'll call them "Tim" and "Sarah"). All of them had seen and heard strange things in the property, and all of them were frightened—particularly the youngest daughter, Katie. It had gotten to the point that she did not want to be in the home anymore and was frightened of her own bedroom. It was mainly for her sake that everyone wished for a speedy resolution concerning the activity in the trailer.

When Terri's group had gotten the call about the place, they had decided to coinvestigate the property with a paranormal group from Florida. During this investigation, one of the investigators claimed to have been touched by an unseen entity and, later that same evening, Tim had "gone into a fit." He claimed to be under assault by a spirit who was trying to possess him. According to the family, this had happened at least one other time.

The family, as well as the Mississippi investigators present, was now wary of the possibility of another possession taking place. Because of this event, Terri wanted to have another, outside researcher present for her group's next investigation of the home.

Witnesses to the previous attack reported that Tim had reacted violently to the affair and had to be physically restrained from attacking the investigators on the scene. I wasn't sure how much of a deterrent I would be for Tim to avoid violence, but I understood why they all wanted to have someone else present. At the very least, I could help with restraining him!

When I asked about the history of activity in the home, Terri explained that there was simply too much information to go into detail about over the phone and that I needed to get down to Mississippi ASAP if I wanted to help out and investigate this case with them the following night. I told her I would be there the following day, but I needed to know (at the very least) the basics of what was happening so I could bring appropriate gear for tackling the investigation. Here's what she told me:

1. The earliest paranormal occurrences at the location involved stones hitting the exterior of the house. When Joanne would go outside to see who was throwing them, nobody would be there. This eventually escalated into an incident that involved deputies from the local sheriff's office coming out to investigate—and they experienced the exact same thing (only the rocks hit their squad cars instead of the home).

2. On at least one occasion, a member of the Martin family was standing in the driveway (talking to a second person) when, instead of a rock, a couple of coins seemed to fall out of thin air. The coins were

all recently minted and seemed perfectly normal according to the witnesses.

3. Residents of the home had heard mysterious scratching noises in the walls and the sounds of disembodied voices. The voices seemed to be male, of an unsettling quality, and they alarmed those who heard them. The scratches seemed to originate from the walls that surrounded the living room and adjoining master bedroom. These were said to start subtly and then escalate to frantic proportions.

4. On at least two occasions, the scents of rotten eggs and feces had suddenly appeared and then disappeared just as quickly. Again, this phenomenon usually occurred in the living room area, though there was at least one instance of this happening in the kitchen (which adjoins the living room).

5. Objects had been witnessed moving by themselves, including utensils flying from the kitchen into the living room. This culminated into one horrific night in the master bedroom. (More on this later.)

6. The male tenant of the spare room (Tim) claimed to have been possessed at least twice by an "evil ghost" they dubbed "John." They thought that John was a malevolent spirit, but did not rule out the possibility that it could also be a demon. This was witnessed

once by the Mississippi and Florida paranormal groups and by the other tenants on another occasion.

7. John was not the only spirit thought to be in the home. They believed there were three ghosts total within the trailer: John, Joanne's ex-husband, and the spirit of a young girl.

But perhaps the most interesting thing I was told about the haunting involved the evening that all the paranormal activity came to a head. This is the story I was told:

Joanne, Julie, Tim, and Sarah were all congregated in the living room, settled in for the night and watching television, when they noticed there was an audible scratching sound coming from the wall that separates that room from the master bedroom. Tim got up to check out the sounds, but they immediately ceased when he approached the wall. This event happened a couple of times before they decided to just ignore the sounds, writing them off as possibly being the product of a rodent.

It was then that a fork suddenly flew into the living room from the direction of the kitchen. The utensil bounced off one of the living room walls and fell in the middle of the carpeted floor before the astonished eyes of all of them. Apparently, whatever was in the trailer didn't like to be ignored!

Fearing that something was "about to happen," they discussed leaving the trailer for a while when a loud commotion suddenly began in the adjoining master bedroom. They listened as the loud sounds of bangs and knocks came from that room. It sounded as if someone was violently moving pieces of furniture back and forth across the floor.

Joanne stood and cautiously approached the doorway to the bedroom; it was then that she witnessed drawers sliding out of the bedroom's dresser and chest of drawers all by themselves. And they didn't just fall on the floor. They flew out of furniture, tumbling end over end, dumping out their contents in a heap onto the bedroom floor.

At this point, the strong scent of rotten eggs filled the air and smoke began to visibly emanate from a small television set in the bedroom. The television then exploded and smoke rolled out in a heavy cloud. Fearing a fire was imminent, Tim ran into the bedroom and grabbed the TV, pitching it right through one of the trailer's front windows into the yard. But the activity wasn't over yet…

According to all those present, the bed mattress then began to violently shake and eventually flipped into the air to land against a wall. The box springs then followed suit. That was when Tim went into hysterics and claimed that he saw a shadowy shape shoot by him. Moments later, he would begin clawing at himself and yelling that something was trying to get into him.

He lashed out at those around him, frightening them all even more, but eventually calmed down when he felt the danger had passed. After that, the activity seemed to come to a sudden halt and life went back to normal in the Martin household. However, because of this evening's events, the family decided to call in the Mississippi paranormal group. The activity was simply too frightening for them to tolerate any more.

Now, fearing that the master bedroom was the habitat of the entity, the family hung a heavy blanket over the doorway that separated that area from the living room and they all decided to only enter that space if it was absolutely necessary. But since that night, they had heard regular "rumbles" come from that empty room. Rumbles that would, literally, shake the entire trailer.

Breaking Down the Phenomena

Several aspects of this case intrigued me right off the bat—the first being the throwing of stones. While much of the reported activity at the Martin home is quite common in paranormal cases, most people do not know about mysterious stone-throwing. This is, however, a phenomenon that is known to investigators.

Author Jerome Clark talks about such "phantom attackers" in his book, *Unexplained!*. He mentions several cases (including a well-documented affair in Chico, California, in 1922) that involved rocks being thrown by invisible hands. Interestingly, local law enforcement would often be involved with these cases as well—and much like the Martin case, they would find no assailants in the area.

According to Clark, this type of activity is usually indicative of a poltergeist type of haunting, and is usually accompanied by other poltergeist symptoms, such as the presence of a young girl, objects moving on their own, and persistent rapping sounds. All of these conditions were present in the Martin home.

The second thing that caught my attention in the case details was the idea of a ghost or spirit possessing the young man. The residents had stated that an entity named "John" was trying to possess Tim—not any demonic being. Though instances of this happening have been documented, they are usually benevolent affairs—incidents that are usually instigated on purpose by the living.

During the great age of Spiritualism, mediums would often allow spirits to temporarily possess/inhabit them in order to converse with the dead (of course most of these so-called Spiritualists and psychics were complete frauds). It was, in fact, quite a popular pastime.

Reports of an "evil" spirit trying to possess a living being, however, are extremely rare—though in cases where this has happened, it was always for a *reason*, which usually involves unfinished business on Earth, wanting to communicate with a family member, or a refusal to simply move on to the afterlife. Spirits of humans rarely possess a living being with the intent of killing the host (unlike possession by a nonhuman, or demon).

The final type of paranormal activity that interested me in the Martin home—and also set off a few internal alarms—was the laundry list of activity in the trailer that is usually associated with demonic infestation (meaning the presence of a demon or nonhuman entity in a home). Things like the scent of feces, persistent scratching sounds, and rumbles in the walls usually make the short list of such activity—not to mention the possessions!

Though I cannot personally vouch for the existence of demons, I do know that some spirits can be downright nasty and do their best to scare the inhabitants of a home (mostly because they are, presumably, defending their territory from encroachment). In many instances, these harmful spirits are often labeled as "demonic" or the equivalent, depending on the religious views of the afflicted. As for the actual existence of demons…well, let's just say the jury is still out as far as I'm concerned, though I do not discount the possibility of such things.

After my discussion with Terri, it was clear that I was about to set foot into a very strange case—a case with several distinct possibilities. Was the Martin family suffering from a particularly intense haunting, an ongoing poltergeist, or were they plagued with demonic infestation? I had no idea, but I intended to find out. Research was sorely needed…

Initial Thoughts

After listening to Terri's story, I knew that three things would have to be investigated immediately. First, I asked Terri to attempt to call the local sheriff's office to confirm the incident when the Martins witnessed rocks hitting the house/vehicles.

Second, I wanted the trailer checked for possible gas leaks. Natural gas can often be mistaken for the smell of rotten eggs and I wanted to rule out the possibility of a mundane explanation for that scent.

Lastly, I wanted a competent plumber to look at the water pipes. When pipes go bad, they can often rattle in the wall. I wanted to be sure that this was not responsible for the rumbles that the family was hearing.

After wrapping up my phone call with Terri, I went over my notes from the conversation and gathered the gear that I would need for my trip into the delta. I packed the usual items for my investigations—digital camera with night vision, digital audio recorders, camcorder with night vision, etc.—but I knew that the most important tool for this trip would be my own experience and senses.

Over the years, I have investigated numerous reputedly haunted places—hotels, museums, private residences, etc. And in my experience, there are significantly more places that pan out to be *mistakenly thought of as haunted* than places that actually are haunted.

Because of this, I stay tuned for specific types of events and tend to pay special attention to the hot spots of a property that inhabitants point out. This is standard operating procedure, and it has saved me countless man-hours by not investigating the wrong places. Even though this was no standard case by any stretch of the imagination, I would take the same logistical approach to the investigation of the Martin property.

Planning my trip and the gear I would take along for the investigation, I was most concerned with the reported possessions. According to Terri, the event was quite disturbing and everyone feared an additional outbreak of violence from Tim. I wondered if he was simply reacting to the proximity of a spirit with a bit of hysteria.

In other words, what if a ghost was approaching him—perhaps even touching him as one investigator previously reported experiencing—and fearing the worst, he was going into a panic and beginning to flail about, thinking he was either *going* to be possessed or that he was in the *process* of being possessed? Certainly most people would be terrified.

I felt it simply had to be this or—to be blunt—he was faking it for whatever reason: attention, insanity, or drug/alcohol influence. Either way, I planned to directly confront him regarding the situation. I would not have him upsetting my chances of performing a thorough and extensive investigation of the property. If he would be unable to control himself in this regard, he would simply have to leave the property for the duration of my visit (once I had finished interviewing him, of course).

I was also disturbed by the fact that the two young girls of the household were often present for the nightmarish activity. Julie was in her early teens, but Katie was only ten years old. This is the kind of environment that can permanently scar the psyche of a young person, and I did not want either of the children to be present during my investigation of the trailer.

Though removing the young girls could possibly risk taking the "battery" for the phenomena out of the equation (most paranormal investigators believe poltergeists happen in the households of young girls because spirits tap them for their prepubescent energy), I did not want to risk any harm to them mentally or physically.

I had little to no time to fully research the specifics of the case, but I thought it best to at least brush up on the basics of demonic infestation and poltergeist activity before driving down to the home the following day. After all, it's better to be prepared than caught off guard, right?

Possession and Demonic Infestation

I can still remember reading the books *The Devil in Connecticut, The Haunted,* and *In a Dark Place* when I was young. All three books were written by different authors, but they all featured cases that were investigated by the infamous husband and wife team of Ed and Lorraine Warren. But, more importantly, all three books scared me to death!

Unlike most paranormal investigations of today, the Warrens' cases seemed to almost always spin off into the realm of the demonic. These stories were as frightening as they were entertaining—but when I read these books today, though, I'm amazed at how much of the reported activity in the cases falls under the simple heading of "haunting." But, then this is just *my* opinion.

During a paranormal investigation, the opinions concerning the activity at a location often influence how a case is ultimately judged. And so it was that the Warrens labeled many of the activities detailed in their cases as being signs of demonic infestation. They believed that the events were of a diabolical nature, so their remedies for coping with the paranormal activity were usually of a religious nature.

In the book *The Haunted* by Robert Curran, the Warrens are quoted describing the four stages of demonic infestation: Infestation, Oppression, Possession, and Death. Of these stages, the hardest to quantify would be the first two. This is because the things that are often cited as signs of infestation are also usually associated with simple hauntings: knocks/raps on the walls, objects moving of their own accord, disembodied voices, etc. And "oppression" has as much to do with the psychological state of the inhabitants of a haunted house as it does with the paranormal activity there. Let me explain…

Let's say, for example, that the aforementioned elements of infestation were happening in a house inhabited by a paranormal enthusiast. In that instance, the inhabitant would be elated at the apparent activity in the household, as well as be thrilled at the prospect of possibly encountering a ghost. So, clearly, this person would not be oppressed in any way.

Conversely, if an inhabitant is terrified by the possibility of a ghost pulling at their bed sheets during the night or speaking into their ear, that individual could definitely feel a bit oppressed by the goings-on in their property without ever really experiencing anything specifically of a demonic nature. When people are frightened, they often jump to the worst possible conclusion—and, so, a ghost suddenly becomes a demon.

As for the third stage of demonic infestation, possession, you really have to realize how murky these waters truly are. Every year, scores of folks from all over the world report being possessed by demons. The vast majority of these turn out to either be frauds, sufferers of a mental disorder, or a hysterical ultrareligious individual who is misinterpreting what's going on around them. Don't believe me? Just check out any of the books by Gabriele Amorth, the official exorcist to the diocese of Rome. He lists many of these cases, as well as cites examples of the rare, real thing.

When the movie *The Exorcist* first hit the movie screens in 1974, it not only terrified thousands of moviegoers, it also spawned an epidemic of sudden possession cases all over the world.

In an article titled "Behavior: Exorcist Fever" in *Time* magazine, Dr. Ari Kiev (a psychiatrist at New York Hospital-Cornell Medical Center) wrote, "If people are attracted to this film, then that is what is in their subconscious. Then again, many patients see themselves as the devil."

The article also tells of the influence the film had on the public, "A prominent Midwest Catholic theologian received dozens of calls from confused people fearful that they were losing their grip on reality. A number of priests reported receiving inquiries from people who believed themselves possessed."

So were all these people under demonic assault? It's more likely that these folks were terrified by something in their lives and were afraid of experiencing the events associated with "Regan" in the movie. Or they were simply people who wanted attention. (Hey, sometimes the obvious reason is the best.) Or maybe these individuals wanted so much to believe in the Devil (as well as God) that they subconsciously *wanted* to be possessed in a way that would provide them with a form of proof that their religion is valid. This line of thinking, in my opinion, could also be applied to the Warren cases.

Were the Warrens simply investigating haunted houses, but their own belief system dictated that they label the affairs as being "demonic?" Maybe. I don't know. I wasn't there. But this could certainly be a possibility. One thing can generally be agreed upon, though: *something* was happening in those cases and evidence needed to be gathered—regardless of the viewpoint of *what* was going on. Looking at the Martin case, I was confronted with the same challenges. Of course there is also the fourth stage of demonic infestation to contend with as well: Death.

Though somebody dying from possession is extremely rare, it has happened. One such case was highlighted in the case and movie titled *The Exorcism of Emily Rose*. The film was based on a real case that happened in Germany in the 1970s.

A young girl by the name of Anneliese Michel was reportedly possessed and underwent a series of intense exorcisms that resulted in her death. Two of the priests involved with the exorcism, as well as the girl's parents, were held accountable for the death and were convicted of negligent manslaughter.

Later it would be revealed that Anneliese was previously diagnosed with mental illness and even suffered a form of epilepsy, so many have questioned whether or not she was, indeed, ever actually possessed. And, unfortunately, though many of the details of the ordeal can be debated, one thing is certain: Anneliese did die.

While researching the particulars of demonic attack, I came across an interesting article written by Bishop Thomas J. Olmsted for *The Catholic Sun* titled "Year for Priests: St. John Vianney, Part Two: The Devil's Attack." In the article, Bishop Olmsted details the demonic harassment that Father John Vianney experienced during his priesthood.

Olmsted states, "In addition to…ordinary ploys, demons resort to other extraordinary acts, on rare occasions, with the same intention of thwarting the plan of God and undercutting our filial trust in Him. These harassments can be of three kinds: infestations, possessions, and obsessions."

Olmsted goes on to detail events that occur during infestation—things like noises, cries, bangs/rattles, and the appearance of apparitions. These were things all reported in the Martin home. Of course, I was already aware of the implications of infestation and possession. It was the second type of activity mentioned by Olmsted, obsession, that caught my eye the most.

Obsession: Part Two

Ever since the first paranormal investigator set foot in the first haunted place, there has been the fear of obsession. This fear, basically put, is that by constantly exposing oneself to the paranormal, as well as studying it and reading about it, one can actually attract spirits and entities. It's thought by many in the paranormal community that the simple act of "obsessing" about the dead can actually cause a person to eventually be visited by such.

Over the years, many researchers have supported this theory by writing about personal experiences while being involved with a haunting—or when investigating paranormal activity. These are experiences that occur in their own homes after returning there from investigating particularly horrific places. While it seems the stuff of horror movies, it does seem to happen on occasion and it can be a negative aspect of becoming a paranormal investigator. In addition, obsession is often reported by investigators in another form as well…

If you investigate the paranormal for any amount of time, you will begin to run into a certain type of client: people who seem to *want to be haunted*. These individuals often watch ghost programs, read books about hauntings, and sometimes even participate in various types of séances and other activities that seem geared toward communicating with the dead.

If the concept of obsession is a valid one, then these particular people may actually be causing their own haunting

by actively obsessing over the subject. And if the ghost enthusiasts are bad about this, then imagine how it can be with
an overly zealous religious person. How many times a day
would that person think about the Devil and/or demons? Or
dwell on the subject of evil?

Could an extreme amount of concern about spirits and
demons actually cause a place to become infested? Or, worse
yet, cause a person to become possessed? Many believe so.
Olmsted writes, "With obsession, the Devil goes beyond
infestations and actually plays on the external senses of
the body or influences a person's memory or imagination."
Think about that for a moment...

For example, let's say you see a dark shadow move
strangely. Because you are already afraid of demonic infestation—and are possibly dwelling on the subject a bit
too much—your memory of the shadow slowly changes.
With time, your memory/imagination will begin to tell
you that what you actually saw was the manifestation of
something demonic or ghostly.

Multiply this event times a hundred in one home and
you can see why obsession can be a dangerous thing. Even
if no entity was "attracted" by all this attention, the act of
obsession could certainly cause a person to become paranoid and emotionally wrecked.

Knowing all of this, it would be important for me to
gauge how tuned in to the paranormal, and possibly demonic subjects, the Martin family was. Maybe their interest in these subjects was affecting how they were looking at

the activity, or perceived activity, in their environment. And I would have to do this without actually bringing up those subjects myself…

Past experience dealing with religious households and their hauntings has taught me to steer clear of any religious suggestions of activity. This is because it can cause investigations to go down strange paths—paths that usually involve clergy and religious ritual.

So I would cautiously avoid bringing up any subject related to demons, exorcism, or infestation with the Martin family. I did not want to have to deal with any requests of performing an exorcism, deliverance, or clearing on my first visit—and, more to the point, I did not want to affect what they would tell me firsthand about what was happening in the home.

Avoiding the subject of the demonic would prove to be no challenge, though, since I only worked with the scientific method. Besides, looking at all the reported activity in the home, there was a lot more happening with this case than is typically associated with infestation. Much of the Martin family's paranormal activity seemed to fall under the heading of "poltergeist."

Elements of a Poltergeist

Usually when the word "poltergeist" is brought into play, yet another movie springs to mind. Though less influential on the psyche of the public than *The Exorcist*, the film has, unfortunately, led a lot of people astray in what they tend to associate with this phenomenon.

Besides the most obvious non-truths (trees snatching kids through windows, clown dolls attacking people, spirits speaking through the television, etc.), the biggest fallacy is perhaps the presence of a ghost at all. These days, most researchers believe that a poltergeist event—often dubbed "PK" by the paranormal community—has more to do with the psychokinetic ability (to move objects solely by mental effort) of an individual than it does with any spirit.

Typically, when a paranormal case is labeled as being a poltergeist, there seems to be a person who lives in the environment that serves as a sort of catalyst to the events happening around them. Sometimes, by simply being present, activity seems to generate around these individuals—though activity is not always limited to this circumstance.

At times, this activity is thought to be the product of an entity present in the home—at other times the activity is thought to actually be initiated by the person in question. In most of these instances, this psychokinetic ability is not even perceived by the person who is doing it. This is because their PK ability is usually a result of traumatic or dramatic changes happening within this person's psyche (such as a sudden life change, a tragic loss, or puberty).

Poltergeist activity almost always includes objects moving of their own accord (in and around the property), as well as finding things relocated in new locations. Sometimes these events are witnessed in real time—including the spontaneous appearance of items—and sometimes the movement is discovered after the fact. Even more perplexing is that fact that, in some cases, these are items that seem to have never existed in the home in the first place (such as foreign objects, antique items, etc.).

On rare occasions, the strength of a poltergeist can actually be so great that heavy/massive items can actually be manipulated. There are examples of this happening in cases like the Bell Witch, the well-documented Enfield poltergeist, and most recently, the infamous "Danny" poltergeist case.

With the Bell Witch—perhaps the most well-known American poltergeist case in history—objects moving of their own accord was a commonplace activity. The Bell family constantly observed household items being thrown across a room, as well as heard constant noises in their home's walls, and even felt invisible hands slapping and pinching them! Activity at the home was so high it was observed by numerous witnesses, including former United States president Andrew Jackson.

More recently, family members involved with the Danny poltergeist also witnessed objects moving in their home. When the Cobb family in Savannah, Georgia, purchased an antique bed at a local auction, they had no idea that they had just inherited a mischievous spirit as well. When young Jason Cobb attempted to sleep in the bed, strange things would happen: a photo of his deceased grandparents would flip down by itself and the boy would feel the pressure of another person sitting/lying on the bed. This activity led the family to experiment with their newfound ghost.

Over the course of the poltergeist—an ongoing incident chronicled by local journalist Jane Fishman of the *Savannah Morning News*—the spirit would move toys from the room onto the bed and even communicate to family members via crayon and paper. It was through these communications that the family learned the spirit was named "Danny" and that he was seven years old. Danny also informed the Cobb family that his mother had perished in the antique bed and that he did not like people sleeping in it.

Investigators on the scene in Savannah would later conclude that Danny wasn't the only spirit in the home; there were, according to them, multiple entities in the property and that they were all a product of the psychic ability of young Jason, coupled with unusually high EMF fields that generated from the boy's bedroom wall.

Was it possible that the events reported in the Martin case were being generated unknowingly by one of the home's inhabitants? While it was possible that at least some of the activity could fall under this heading, it was clear that definitely not all of the activity could be. For instance, there's no way to psychically produce a scent or disembodied voice in a room—though both of these activities have occurred during poltergeists that were associated with an entity being present.

So, while I would have to look at the possibility of there being poltergeist activity in the home, the investigation would not end with that. But, again, the rock-throwing aspect of the case intrigued me quite a bit. If they were faking any of the activity there—or simply lying about it—why would they choose a paranormal event that's unknown to most people?

Famed investigator Guy Lyon Playfair wrote of just such an event in his book *This House Is Haunted—An Investigation of the Enfield Poltergeist*. He wrote, "Stones fall onto your kitchen floor, as if they had come through the ceiling. Somebody, or something, starts banging on the wall. Things disappear, and reappear somewhere else. Before long, you realize it can't be an earthquake, or the Concorde, or mice. It must be something else—something entirely inexplicable and very frightening indeed."

Planning My Investigation

Clearly I would have to be open to whatever was going to happen in the Martin home during my visit. I would interview the family members, get as much history as possible concerning the land and the family, and then attempt to capture as much activity as possible on audio/video. My chief concern was the possibility of another possession—or the family spiraling into a state of hysteria.

Since one of the members of Terri's group had been touched by an entity, and there was a significant amount of activity reported, I was confident that something paranormal was going on in the Martin home—it would just be a matter of figuring out what that "something" was and bringing about some type of resolution for all involved.

I also began looking for an area clergy who might be willing to perform a blessing on the house; if the Martin family was at all religious (and this subject came up despite me avoiding it), this might put them at ease about living in such an environment. So I packed up my gear, gassed up my truck, and prepared for a long drive into the hot, steamy Mississippi delta…

3

THE INITIAL VISIT

I met the folks from the Mississippi paranormal team at their local McDonald's. They were wolfing down Big Macs and mentally preparing for an evening of intense investigation. Once the hellos were taken care of, they promptly told me that I should use the bathroom at the restaurant since the one at the Martin home was in extremely poor condition—and that I should fuel up for a long and grueling evening of paranormal activity.

As I worked my way through my meal, they warned me that Tim had apparently had another episode with possession and that I should be on my toes. The entire Mississippi team would be accompanying me for the evening (Terri, Patricia, Tom, and Blake), so if it became necessary to restrain Tim, we would certainly be able to do so.

Since Tom was the biggest guy in their group (and much bigger than me), I pulled him to one side and mentioned, "You may have to play tough guy tonight if Tim starts acting up. I plan to confront him about all this possession stuff—and I don't want it ruining the investigation."

He nodded, but I knew he had to be wondering why I was taking this approach. Provincial thinking was that possession was beyond the control of those being afflicted. Instinct told me, however, that this was most likely not the case with Tim. I was convinced that he was either faking the incidents to get attention or he was paranoid and panicking. I was just hoping that telling Tim to buck up and be strong might be enough to keep him from freaking out.

Once we finished up at the restaurant, we drove the twenty minutes or so into the "boonies" to the Martin trailer. And when I say boonies, I mean boonies. The trailer was located against a massive expanse of forest, far from what could even be termed as a "small town." This was about as rural as we could get.

During the ride, I was told that the vast, wooded area surrounding the Martin trailer was once a popular place for local lynchings and other unsavory crimes around the turn of the century. It was safe to say that this was probably not mentioned in any of the local travel brochures ...

Since we were speaking about crimes, I asked Terri if they had managed to speak to the local sheriff's office to validate the claims of mysterious stones hitting their squad cars. She said they had not, so I made a mental note to make the call myself upon my return home. If even one deputy could confirm that he/she had witnessed rocks being thrown at a squad car—and nobody had been seen or found in the vicinity doing it—it would go a long way toward corroborating Joanne's story.

Soon, we found ourselves winding our way down an old gravel road and then up an old, washed-out driveway to the Martin property. Despite several warnings—and a generous mental picture—words could not have prepared me for the level of destruction at this home.

Signs of the family's old, original homestead were still on the property, including a ramshackle shed that stood just outside the trailer and rusted pieces of old tin roof strewn about the yard that had once protected an early family home. The trailer itself had also seen better days, but seemed structurally sound—though the gaping hole where a window once was said otherwise.

As I made my way across the yard, I paused to snap a quick photo of a broken television set that lay in the yard. I assumed this was the TV that had smoked, then exploded, during the largest episode of paranormal activity in the trailer. Terri had mentioned that Tim had thrown the set through a window (where the gaping hole now was?) to get it out of the home. I stopped and knelt in the grass to examine it more closely.

There was a perfect round hole in the television's screen with cracks radiating out as if it had, indeed, exploded as the Martins claimed—or like the screen had, perhaps, been shot by a small gun. I peered inside the hole and noted that there were signs that a fire had burned within the television, too. Black and burnt tubes, wires, etc., were still present behind the screen. After I was finished with the TV, I stood and took a long look around the property.

In addition to the shed and a few random household items scattered about the yard, there was also what appeared to be a long-abandoned car in the driveway. It was apparent that Joanne and her family had had some hard times—and that ghosts were not the only concern they lived with in the wilds of Mississippi. I hoped the interior of the trailer would prove to be different than the rustic exterior. And as soon as I walked into the trailer, I realized it was, indeed, much different: the inside was far worse.

With the help of Terri and Patricia, Joanne had cleaned up a bit in the living room to prepare for my visit, but the rest of the trailer stood in a state of massive disarray. Several rooms contained mountains of random clothing, junk, and papers; the kitchen held the remains of numerous meals past; and the carpets were tracked with months of stains and mildew—and these were not the rooms that had been, reportedly, trashed by the entity! With the exception of the living room, there wasn't an organized area in the entire place.

I mentally noted the closest tree to the house, intending to take the group's advice to dodge the bathrooms there. As I looked around, I was suddenly saddened by the knowledge that two young girls were living in this place. How could they stand it? Patricia then called from the kitchen for me; the family was ready to meet the new investigator.

After entering, I was quickly introduced to Joanne, Tim, and Sarah. The two girls, Julie and Katie, were not present for my investigation per my request. Joanne was in her late fifties, while Tim and Sarah were in their twenties. Sarah said little to nothing during my entire visit, though she did back up many of the claims made concerning activity there with a brief nod. Tim, on the other hand, had plenty to say.

He spoke about the ghosts, about the area in general, and about any other random subject that came to mind. Words spilled out of his mouth in a quick jumble that instantly made me think that he was a drug addict waiting for his next fix. As he spoke, I found it hard to make eye contact with him, so as my eyes drifted, I noticed a shakily scrawled, prison-blue tattoo glaring from his arm with the blazon "Hot Boy" written there. I would later learn that he did, indeed, get this in jail. Apparently he was quite popular there…

Terri and Patricia then gave me a thorough tour of the trailer that culminated with a walk through the master bedroom. Not wanting to alter anything, the room still stood in the state of disaster that resulted from the entity's temper tantrum. Though Terri had told me all about what had happened there, nothing could have prepared me for the mess. If this room had been torn up by a spirit, I dreaded running into him/her. It looked like a war zone. I snapped a few photos and decided to spend what little bit of daylight we had left interviewing Joanne Martin about their ordeal in the property.

More Details of the Haunting

Though Joanne lived, literally, in the middle of nowhere, she was still quite social and wanted to talk about what was happening in her home. She introduced me (again) to Tim and Sarah, the tenants of the spare bedroom, and informed me that her two daughters were staying with relatives who lived in the vicinity if I needed to speak to them.

I told Joanne that I would, indeed, like to speak to Julie, the eldest daughter, at some point, but I was most interested in interviewing her and listening to her story. So after switching on an audio recorder that I had in my pocket, I managed to get the details of her haunting firsthand.

She and the rest of her family believed that there were three ghosts in the trailer. The first was a male entity by the name of "Keith." He was the father of one of Joanne's children, Julie, and he had recently passed away of natural causes. According to Joanne, the family had originally believed their stone-throwing entity to be Keith (when he was still alive); Joanne and he had gone through a bad breakup and she suspected that he was staking out the trailer to terrorize her as punishment for giving him the boot. Then he died.

When the rocks continued to routinely pummel the place, it became painfully obvious that Keith was not responsible—or at least he had taken his new hobby with him beyond the grave. Either way, the entire family now believed that Keith watched over the trailer and his daughter, Julie. So, long story short, he was thought of as a benevolent spirit in the home. As far as I was concerned, this was good news. So far, all I had heard about ghosts from Terri was that the place was inhabited by an angry spirit, so this was a breath of fresh air.

The second entity in the home was also, strangely enough, associated with Julie. According to the girl, she had been seeing and hearing the spirit of a young girl dubbed "Emily" since she was very young. Emily would visit her in her bedroom and often told her when things going awry in the trailer were the product of the other two ghosts.

Typically, when activity would start ramping up in the household, Emily would disappear—almost as if she was hiding from the other two spirits. I found this to be quite interesting.

In cases of infestation that I had researched, entities would often pretend to be someone harmless in order to gain the trust of those who lived in the house—for often nefarious reasons. The fact that Emily would "disappear" when the other spirits would be appearing and performing activity suggested that this could be a possibility in the Martin household.

Of the third spirit in the trailer, an entity the residents called "John," little was known. Joanne claimed that John was a black man who had once lived in the area that was "done wrong" by one of Joanne's relatives (meaning he was most likely killed). Knowing the racially charged background of this area of Mississippi, I found this story to be plausible, if a little sketchy and devoid of detail.

When I asked her for more information, she stated that anything to do with John was just rumor that she had heard growing up—though there were some mean men in her family over the years who certainly could have done any number of horrible deeds to such a person.

According to Joanne, it was John that would become violent and attempt to possess Tim. As Terri indicated in our first phone call, it did seem that the Martins were claiming that a human spirit was possessing Tim. Knowing that we would talk more about the subject of ghosts, I decided to move on to some background information regarding the Martin family and the area.

Background of the Case

As mentioned above, Joanne and Keith had recently undergone a divorce, so initially she thought a lot of the activity that they now know to be of a paranormal nature was being perpetrated by Keith—after all, he was still making attempts to reconcile with the rest of the family and was angry with Joanne for rebuffing his advances. This activity included the strange rocks that would hit the home—as well as strange knocks and bangs that would originate from the walls (possibly from outside).

Though the land had been in their family for several generations, they had purchased and placed their brand-new trailer on the property in 2000 and, at the time, Joanne lived there with her four daughters and Keith. They divorced a short time later, and soon after that they began to hear stones hitting the sides and roof of the trailer. Joanne would open the door and yell into the darkness for Keith to leave them alone, but the attacks would continue—sometimes all night long, much to the dismay of the children.

After Keith passed away in 2003, activity in the trailer slowed to a crawl. It remained this way until the family briefly fled the home in 2005 as Hurricane Katrina pummeled the area. But after they returned to the trailer, they began to witness significantly more paranormal events.

The rock-throwing became more prevalent and they started noticing things were magically appearing in the home—this includes the incident that involved coins dropping out of thin air. Over the years, as activity became more and more frequent, the family became sort of accustomed to things happening there—especially since young Julie had already begun communicating with the spirit of Emily at this point.

I asked if anyone else had ever seen or heard Emily. Joanne quickly told me a story that involved an overnight stay by a couple of Julie's friends. During that evening, the three girls were sitting in Julie's bedroom having a good time, when one of the guests suddenly screamed and pointed at the bedroom window.

She had seen a pale, young female face peering in, watching the girls. A face that did not seem quite right…Julie informed the startled girls that this was just the spirit of Emily, who was hiding outside because she did not know her guests. Needless to say, this was probably the last overnight stay in the trailer for either of those young girls!

Since several people had seemingly seen the ghost of Emily, I asked what the spirit looked like. Joanne promptly stated that she was a young girl, about four feet tall, and wearing a white dress. I asked, "Has anyone been able to note any details about the girl herself—not what she's wearing?"

Joanne answered, "She's a little white girl with long, blonde hair." Good enough. Joanne would go on to reiterate that Julie had the most experience with Emily and that she could give me a lot more information about that spirit. I noted this and we moved on to more of the history within the trailer.

As previously stated, the paranormal events seemed to really start happening after the family returned home following Hurricane Katrina—and it was also when the family began to fear being in the place. This is when Joanne decided to rent out the spare bedroom. I guess she figured, quite reasonably, that she would feel safer if another adult was living there with her family. That was when Tim and Sarah moved in.

Interestingly, almost all the information regarding the presence of a spirit named John came from Tim. He stated that when he was possessed by the spirit, he could communicate with him. And it wasn't just John. During one attack, he said he could also channel/communicate with Keith.

According to Joanne, Tim described Keith perfectly (even though he had never met him or seen any photographs) and that he had even made a reference to a favorite shirt that Keith had lost in the trailer. As Joanne was feeding me all of this information, Tim and Sarah stood as a strange chorus of sorts, nodding and repeating "uh-huh" behind her. It seemed that they all agreed on the story at least. But I had to wonder even more about Tim now.

Though it was clear that activity was occurring prior to him moving in, it was also obvious that Tim was at least escalating the feelings of anxiety and hysteria in the home. All of them lived in fear of his bouts of possession. In order for me to have a productive investigation, I did not want any such environment. It would be a massive distraction and, possibly, even make some of the residents and investigators to want to leave.

So I decided to make my bold move regarding these possessions: I approached Tim, pulled him to the side, and told him, "Listen up, tonight I'm investigating this house. There's not going to be any of this possession crap going on."

To my amazement, he simply nodded and said, "There won't be. The last time John tried to get me, I told him 'no more' and he has stopped." Huh? I was taking a big chance at possibly upsetting everyone there to even try this approach, but I figured if he still had an episode despite my warning it would just show that it was beyond his means to stop the phenomena—but if he simply obliged me, then it would be clear he was faking the whole thing. This "agreement" with John sort of voided my test. I was miffed by this, but, hey, at least there would be no possessions happening that night!

Further questioning of Tim and Sarah revealed other paranormal activity as well. According to the couple, the sounds of voices/growls were often heard while they were watching television in the living room and that objects had moved in that area on several occasions (including the utensil that flew from the kitchen). They also mentioned experiencing sudden headaches and feeling an occasional overwhelming "hot spot" hit them like a swirling blast of hot air.

Joanne also mentioned at least one occasion in which a clock changed time by itself; she had just noted the time and the clock was correct, then a short time later it was suddenly off by several hours, but was still running perfectly. This happened the evening the Mississippi and Florida paranormal groups were performing their investigation—the same investigation where a researcher felt someone touch her with invisible hands.

When I asked Joanne what bothered her the most about the haunting, she stated she was angry about her dogs. Apparently, her pets had been driven off by the entities. No evidence of their whereabouts had ever turned up, and she suspected that they might even be dead.

Joanne had suffered watching her children be terrorized by an evil spirit, endured the almost total destruction of her only home, witnessed her friend/tenant as he underwent horrific episodes of apparent possession—and now she was telling me that her pets, too, had either disappeared, been killed, or were driven off by a malevolent spirit in the trailer. All these negative experiences were almost more than any one person could endure. It was enough for me to ask Joanne something I'd sworn to avoid.

Before wrapping up the interview and diving headfirst into the investigation, I asked Joanne if she would like to have her house blessed. She appeared to be genuinely upset by a lot of the activity in the trailer, so I hoped that this might make her feel better about being there.

She quickly said yes, though she avoided mentioning any particular denomination or religion for the blessing.

When I asked her who she would like to do the blessing, she lit up. "Oh, I believe in it all," she said with a huge smile.

The First Investigation

Now that the preliminaries were over with, it was time to get down to business. Trucks were unloaded, household furniture was rearranged to accommodate movement in complete darkness, and the heat/air-conditioning unit was silenced so that it would not interfere with audio devices. Video cameras and audio recorders were then strategically placed throughout the premises.

Once we had extinguished all the lights in the trailer, we were then able to turn on all the night-vision cameras and kick off our investigation. Gear was distributed throughout the team and the residents were informed to stay quiet and out of the way during our visit. The Mississippi investigators gathered to plan their approach for the evening as I took a few moments to go through a few preliminary steps.

After taking some base readings throughout the house (EMF levels, temperature, etc.), I then took an extensive number of reference photographs, covering almost every inch of the place. I would turn to these photos if I needed to see the original position of a particular item, piece of furniture, or whatever during my review back home. During this photographic trip around the trailer, I noted some strange things.

First off, there seemed to be a lot of magic/occult-oriented items about the home, including small bottles of herbs (marked with their own magical attributes), a small wand carved with symbols that were unfamiliar to me, and some sort of ward/mandala that was drawn on paper and tacked onto the wall. This disturbed me in a small way.

It was one thing to say your home is simply "haunted," but it's quite another thing altogether if you are actually performing rituals and/or attempting to conjure something. I made it a point to ask Joanne about these things. In the meantime, I simply noted (and photographed) the unfamiliar items and continued my walkthrough.

Soon I was confronted with an even more disturbing discovery. Along with the magical paraphernalia, there was also paraphernalia of a different sort: drugs. At least one person in the home was engaging in casual drug use. While this might not have been the case for the majority of the inhabitants—or even explain the ghostly happenings—it definitely meant eyewitness accounts would have to be taken with a grain of salt.

In addition to documenting the environment, walking through the trailer also allowed me to smell for natural gas. There were no signs of the telltale odor, and though this did not completely rule out a leak, it did mean the egg scent that they had smelled was probably from a different source, since the scent would still be present if there was a leak.

Once we had our base readings and everything had been photographed for posterity, we then placed some environmental monitoring devices (digital thermometers, EMF detectors, etc.) strategically within the trailer and took up positions throughout the property to wait for activity. I thought it best to start the night at "ground zero" because of the events reported there, so I took up a vigil in the master bedroom along with Terri of the Mississippi group.

While Patricia, Tom, and Blake staked out various other hot spots in the trailer, Terri and I did some EVP work in the bedroom. Again, this is an attempt to record ghostly voices on our audio recorders. This is done by asking questions and then waiting for a reasonable amount of time for an answer.

Typically, these answers are not heard right after asking the questions, but appear later when listening to the audio during the review. On occasion, if the haunting or entity is strong enough, the answers can even be heard as a disembodied voice in real time during the investigation, though this is actually a rare event.

Making ourselves comfortable, I ran through the usual EVP questions: Is there anybody here with us? Can you make a noise for us? And so forth. As I mentioned in the prologue, it was after I asked, "How long have you been here in this house?" that IT happened. A long, loud rumble coursed throughout the room, shaking the walls around us. I blinked in disbelief and looked over at Terri. She was sitting, eyes wide, looking for anything that might have caused this to happen.

Tom and Blake then came crashing into the room to see what the noise was. Shaking off the surprise of something actually happening, I asked Tom if he had ever heard anything like this before. Though he thought it unlikely, he suggested trying to re-create the sound by messing with the trailer's plumbing.

The underside of the structure was completely open to the elements, so he was concerned that maybe an animal had bumped into the pipes beneath the place. I thought it was worth checking out, though I could not imagine any plumbing-oriented noises that could create the sound that I had just heard. Joanne, pleased that something had happened with new witnesses present, watched as Tom went outside to check everything out.

To that end, he crawled under the trailer and proceeded to shake and bang on various pipes while the rest of us listened inside the trailer. Nothing was even close to the sound we had heard. I had an audio recorder in the room, so I knew the sound of the rumble was definitely captured by the device—along with, hopefully, some good EVPs. I noted the time of the event in a small notebook and waited for Tom to come back inside.

When he returned, Tom stated that although there was nothing under the home to account for the sound we had heard, there was evidence of animals living under the trailer.

This could explain some of the knocks and bangs the family had heard on a regular basis—and possibly even be where her missing pets were taking refuge on occasion. But, again, it did not explain the rumble we had all just heard.

Now the air surrounding this investigation was considerably different. Suddenly everything Joanne had said during the interview carried the weight of possibility. As a result, everyone was now motivated to experience even more activity. So we all switched into high gear and continued.

Several of us stuck around in the bedroom, attempting to get some interaction from any entity that might be present, while the remainder of the team went into the room with the magical items. We were about an hour into investigating in the master bedroom when another strange thing happened.

I had just asked anyone there in the bedroom to "make their presence known" when a loud metal-on-metal clang was heard from right beside me. Startled, I fumbled for a light and quickly looked around the room. The only metal object in my vicinity was an electric radiator/portable heater that was lying on its side on the floor, directly in front of me.

Upon closer examination, I noticed that an old gold watch was now lying on it. It had not been there before. I know this because I had actually sat on the radiator and used it as a makeshift seat for a good while. I carefully picked up the watch and took it with me into the living room.

When I held up the watch for everyone to see, Joanne informed me that she had never seen the watch before in her life. According to her, it wasn't her watch—or anybody else's in the house. Strange. Much like the mysterious materializing coins, it seemed that the old watch had spontaneously appeared in the bedroom—and where it came from, nobody knew.

Luckily this had happened a mere foot in front of my face, albeit in a darkened room. A surveillance camera (with night-vision capability) hooked up to a DVR system was recording in the bedroom, so I hoped the materialization was caught on video. It would be a great piece of evidence if the act had been recorded. Again, I noted the event and the time in my pocket notebook.

Both of these events had happened early in the investigation, so all of us were now quite excited. What was next? The answer: not much. As is true with most paranormal cases, when you want something to happen, it usually doesn't. We would go on and spend hours doing EVP work, roaming room to room with cameras and camcorders, coaxing spirits to do anything to let us know we weren't alone. Unfortunately, only one other unexplainable thing would happen during this trip to the trailer.

I was making my way down the hallway that runs past the children's bedrooms when I thought I saw a black shape shift ahead in the darkness. It appeared to move quickly from the hallway into a side room.

I know from past experiences that these events usually pan out to just be a trick of the light and/or my eyes attempting to adjust to a different level of darkness. On the chance that this was neither of these things, I moved quickly into the area where I saw the shadow go. This was the youngest daughter's (Katie) bedroom.

Moving into this room, I again saw the strange black mass shift—this time toward a closet. I was now sure this was no natural shadow. Whipping out a K2-style EMF detector, I walked toward the closet door. EMF stands for "electromagnetic field" and most paranormal researchers believe that spirits, in order to exist, must give off this type of energy. As a result, carrying a plethora of assorted EMF detectors during an investigation is a ghost hunting standard.

As I slowly crept toward the closet door, I stared at the device in my hand. It was when I reached the outside of the door that the K2 lit up like the Fourth of July. It had picked up an unusually strong reading—but only for a moment. Then it died completely. During our walkthrough of the trailer, we had found no EMF levels above 1.0 milligauss (and this is natural since even well-insulated wiring can give off a low EMF reading), but here there had been a short, sustained spike that literally maxed out the detector.

Though I would spend the next fifteen minutes trying to figure out what caused the spike—or where the possible entity may have gone—the single occurrence was all that happened. The EMF detector would pick up nothing else out of the ordinary and I would see no more strange shadows.

After hours of nothing else of paranormal significance happening, the night began to wear on me and the other investigators. At one point, I took a lap throughout the trailer to check in on the Mississippi team and was greeted by sets of bleary eyes and yawns. Blake was actually asleep on the living room couch, still clutching an audio recorder. It seemed that nothing more of note was going to happen this evening.

In the living room, Joanne wrung her hands with worry. She couldn't understand why "nothing was happening." I explained to her that this sometimes happened when new people came into a place and that it's common to think nothing is happening during an investigation, but then discover later during a review of our audio and video surveillance that we did, indeed, have something paranormal going on. This was when Joanne said something that completely took me by surprise.

A Demonic Moth and a Practical Joke

I had just taken a seat on the couch when Joanne stated that she did not understand why nothing was happening in the trailer since a "demon" was watching us "right now." This was the first mention of anything to do with a demon or anything religious, so it immediately struck me as an odd thing for her to say. Cautiously, I took a look around the trailer. Nothing seemed amiss.

When I asked her where this demon was, she pointed at the wall directly over my head. Cautiously, I peeked in that direction. There was a moth that was perched on the wall just above me. "Huh?" I asked to make sure. "You mean the moth?"

She nodded. "It likes to watch us." Simply put, I was dumbstruck. I had no idea of what to say to this. I struggled to hold my tongue and suppressed the urge to swat the insect dead. Instead, I nodded politely and asked Tom and company to take a walk outside with me. This had to be discussed.

Though I had experienced several unexplainable things over the course of the evening, and it was apparent that paranormal activity was actually happening on the property, I now had serious misgivings concerning the veracity of Joanne Martin. Could she simply be paranoid and actually believe she is under constant surveillance? And why was she suddenly talking about a demon being in the trailer? And, more to the point, why a moth?

I was discussing this very subject with Tom and Blake when Joanne came outside with the remaining members of the team. As the women talked about the lack of activity in the trailer, I saw Blake reach into his pocket and grin. He held out three or four coins in his hand for us to see, and then he snuck around the backside of the inoperable car in the driveway. I groaned as I realized what he was about to do—re-create the materializing coins incident—but then decided to let him do it.

The way I figured it was this: when he tossed the coins into the air to drop in front of Joanne, she would be startled to find money that "materialized" in front of her—which would beg the question, "If this has happened before in the past, why are you so surprised?" Of course, when Blake threw the coins into the air, the exact opposite happened.

After settling in behind the car, Blake quickly flipped the coins into the air. They landed right at the feet of the astonished group talking outside the front door. Terri and Patricia immediately reacted with surprise and excitement. Joanne and Tim barely blinked an eye. Joanne picked up one of the quarters, handed it over to Patricia, and said, "See? This just keeps happening."

While Tom and Blake struggled to control their laughter, I found myself even more perplexed. With such a complete lack of surprise, it was obvious to me that they had experienced this very thing before and were not lying about the previous incidents involving materializing coins and rocks.

I could feel my head beginning to throb…Everything was getting quite confusing and it was becoming harder and harder to know what was fabrication and what was truth concerning this case.

Wrapping It Up

With the night waning and activity that had (apparently) ceased, we decided to wrap up the evening's investigation. We gathered up the gear, said our goodbyes, and drove back into town. For me, it was only the beginning of a very long drive back to Memphis. During this ride, I would mentally assess everything that had happened during the investigation.

On the one hand, I had experienced activity in the master bedroom for myself (there was the loud rumble and the materializing watch) and witnessed a massive black shape move into one of the children's bedrooms. This had been corroborated by the large spike on the EMF detector.

On the other hand, it was apparent that not everything happening in the trailer was of a paranormal nature—there was clearly an element of hysteria that managed to turn things as mundane as a moth flying into the room into a thing of ominous portent. Of course, it could also just have been wishful thinking or desperation on Joanne's part to prove her case. Either way, I had a hard time believing I had encountered a demonic moth.

And on top of this, there was clear evidence of drug use, as well as articles used for magical/ritual purposes. Maybe the Martin family actually *wanted* something to happen in their home—and that, coupled with their obsession with ghosts and the occult had attracted something to them. Something that was pretending to be a little girl named Emily or Julie's dead father. Or maybe even John...whoever that was.

It was all very confusing for my extremely sleepy head, but any way it went, I would have to go over the audio, photographic, and video evidence from this investigation very carefully. The results would have to be the deciding factor that would help form my final opinion as to whether or not the place was, indeed, haunted.

As I drove the seven or so hours back to Tennessee, I went over several past cases that I had conducted along with the other members of Paranormal Inc. Perhaps there was an experience or lesson learned from a previous case that I could draw upon for guidance. There have certainly been moments of enlightenment and, of course, terror over the years...

4

WAR STORIES

The road trip back to Tennessee was long and boring—perfect for doing some thinking and reminiscing. As I mentioned earlier (probably several times), personal experience can make a huge difference in just how a paranormal case is investigated and interpreted. And I was convinced that, despite the outright challenges of the Martin case, there would be past instances that could help me discern what was what in this investigation.

For most investigators, personal experience can often determine the verdict concerning the disposition of a haunting—and whether a place is even haunted at all. The problem can be, though, that different people have different experiences, so oftentimes there can be multiple opinions concerning a haunting (or lack of) and various ways to approach investigating it.

Personal experiences are also essential because they teach investigators important lessons in the field—some basic, some more advanced and unique. Things you would have never known had you not gone out and visited a place for yourself. Despite the plethora of information available about the paranormal, nothing beats actually working on location with clients and capturing evidence for yourself.

Since the formation of my investigative group Paranormal Inc, my team has explored hundreds of unique locations—state parks, battlefields, hotels, restaurants, bed-and-breakfasts, museums…well, you get the idea. And no two investigations have been the same. At least that has been the case when the place has actually been haunted!

If a location is *not* haunted, it's pretty much like every other investigation that goes nowhere: boring. You can probably imagine how much fun is involved with sitting in a silent, dark place and having a conversation with nobody for hours on end. It's the kind of situation that often drives paranormal wannabes back to watching ghost hunters on television instead of actually doing it. But visiting places without hauntings is extremely important to researchers in the field.

An investigator has to learn what constitutes paranormal activity and what does not. Ever notice how people on paranormal television programs always seem to encounter a ghost and how they always appear to be in an actual haunted location? Well, it's not like that in real life. In real life, finding a real haunt is a rare and exhilarating thing—but it does happen on occasion.

And there are always lessons to be learned and personal experiences to be had when you investigate these real places. As I went over some of my past investigations in my head while driving (always with my eyes on the road!), I just knew that there were some past cases that could help me with the Martins.

Devil's Backbone

One of the hardest things for new paranormal groups to do is to get their first real case. As a result, most first-timers usually end up doing a public, outside location. We (Paranormal Inc) were no different. Though Mike and I had already been investigating the paranormal off and on for many years, actually doing a case by the book and working as a formal investigative group would be a new experience for us, so we wanted to do it right.

Since we wanted to avoid going to any local cemetery (nobody dies in a cemetery and who would want to haunt one?), Mike, Brandon, and I researched haunted places in and around southeast Missouri for some time before deciding to make Devil's Backbone Park our first investigation. And in retrospect it seemed a perfect choice.

We had several reasons for choosing this particular location: it was reasonably close by in southwest Illinois, it had a great reputation for having regular paranormal activity, and information about the haunting and the site was readily available on the internet (though the actual history of the area was rather scarce).

Also, it appeared that the haunted area in question was relatively small, which was important. Since we only had a limited amount of gear between the three of us (buying all that electronic equipment is expensive!), we wanted to investigate a place small enough for us to cover with our handful of audio and video recorders. We also wanted a place that three investigators could manage with ease—possibly working well into the night. Devil's Backbone was a perfect fit.

Once we decided on this location, the three of us gathered to discuss how we would approach the case. Logistically, it would pose no real challenge. It was a mere two hours from Cape Girardeau, Missouri (our home base), to Grand Tower, Illinois, and it was a public place, so we would not need to get any special permission from anyone to visit. The only issue I could imagine springing up involved the hours of operation.

Most state and national parks close relatively early and we wanted nighttime to investigate so we could use our nifty new night-vision-capable camcorders. If the park closed at sunset, like many do, we would only get a limited time in the dark there before having to leave. Unfortunately, the park's website did not tell the hours of operation. But I did notice that they had camping.

My thoughts were that, worst-case scenario, we might have to purchase a campsite (even though we would not be camping that night) so that we could stay a few extra hours in the park after dark. This would also give use the option of an all-night investigation. We were pumped up and ready for our first case, so we would most likely be fueled up on adrenaline all night anyway! We just hoped that our limited amount of electronic equipment could handle that much data.

Next, we talked about the actual case. Devil's Backbone was known throughout southern Illinois as a haunted place, so finding details about the ghost(s) was no challenge. The problem was that most of the information from the websites all said the same couple of things! Most of the tales seemed to be of two varieties.

The most common story told about the old rocky ridge overlooking the Mississippi River concerns the ghost of a young girl. During its heyday, Devil's Backbone was known for its iron furnaces and workers would flock there from all over the country for meager pay and dangerous work. The girl was the daughter of the foundry boss who lived in a small stone house in the vicinity of the furnaces.

It's said that this girl fell in love with a migrant worker, and that after her father found out about the crush, the worker was persuaded to quit his job and to move away from the area. As a result, the girl's heart was broken and she pined away the remainder of her days until she died—either from grief or from an unspecified natural cause.

Today, the ruins of the old foundry house can still be found in the wooded area just outside the campground (though some say it is nothing of the sort, but just a random abode that someone lived in sometime over the years). It is this spot that's said to be visited by the ghost of the young girl. She is usually seen in and around the ruins of the house and residents/visitors have reported hearing her screams of anguish in the night.

The second story concerning spirits at Devil's Backbone involves the generally sinister reputation the area had for many years. Besides the fact that the cliffs were often dangerous to those traveling along the river, the location was typically used by river pirates to swoop down on unsuspecting people. Because of this, the area is said to have had a large quantity of murders, robberies, assaults, and crimes in general. Many believe that the misty spirits that are often seen wandering the cliffs are the souls of these poor victims.

Either way, we knew exactly where we needed to go—the top of the cliffs and the area around the foundry house ruins. On paper, it seemed that this would be a simple and straightforward case—but, of course, nothing is ever simple and straightforward!

After we had packed all of our gear and gotten on the road, we learned our first lesson concerning investigating an outdoor location: always check the weather. As we crossed the Mississippi River, clouds were already gathering in the sky and it was fast become apparent that we were in for a large storm that evening. Suddenly we no longer needed a campsite; our time at the location would clearly be limited.

Once we arrived at the park, we managed to spot the landmarks that would lead us to the infamous cliff and foundry house, so we quickly parked, grabbed our gear, and trudged through the brush and trees to the reputedly haunted area. This brings us to lesson learned number two: it was a much harder and longer trek than we imagined. We should have given ourselves more time and left Missouri earlier.

With barely a smear of daylight remaining in the sky—partially because it was getting late, partially because of the incoming storm—we eventually located the ruins and set up some audio and video recorders. I made a mental note to allow more time for travel in the future. (What if there had been a client anxiously awaiting us? We would have appeared unprofessional by cutting it so close.)

After our surveillance of the ruins was in place, we then slowly circled the cliff tops to take some photographs and to do some EVP work. Finally, we were starting to feel like real ghost hunters! But this feeling of elation would be short-lived. We were a whopping forty-five minutes into the investigation when a massive bolt of lightning came crashing out of the sky! So, frustrated and fearing for our lives, we made a mad dash to grab all of our gear before the rain hit and destroyed all of our electronic gear.

Once all of our equipment was gathered, we sprinted through the first torrents of cold rain to our nice, warm vehicle and quickly loaded up. Moments later, we were back on the road. With a few laughs and some jokes about Murphy's Law, we assessed our first "investigation" as we drove back to Missouri.

On the positive side, we had gathered forty-five minutes of audio and video footage, taken approximately a hundred digital photos, and had learned a couple of valuable lessons. On the negative side, we had *only* gathered about forty-five minutes of audio and video footage and our investigation was possibly the shortest ever conducted by a formal paranormal team.

Many people would have been frustrated by all of this—and may have even been tempted to ditch the entire case. But we still treated the footage we had gathered as something to be seriously scrutinized—besides, we needed to practice reviewing audio and video footage anyway. Much to our surprise, we were rewarded with a couple of interesting pieces of evidence.

Though the audio and video recorders had not been running for very long, both devices located at the foundry ruins contained some interesting tidbits. The audio recorder captured a couple instances of what sounded like a female screaming! Since we were always in the immediate area and had not heard any such sounds for ourselves, this was an interesting find. It also matched up with the tales that are told about the old ruins.

In addition, the camcorder that was set a mere two feet from the audio recorder also captured something. For a brief second, a strange blob of visible light appeared in the frame of the video and, just as quickly, disappeared. It was clearly not one of our flashlights (these appeared quite differently on video and can be seen moving through the trees in the background) and we had seen no other lights that evening. Also, the sounds of the female screams were present on the camcorder, too, which indicated to us that these were probably audible sounds (perhaps even a disembodied voice) and not an EVP.

Obviously, we were all elated that our first "case" had gone so well. Despite being in the location for less than an hour, we had walked away with our first paranormal evidence. And this taught us perhaps the most important lesson learned yet: always take an investigation seriously and use your time wisely. Because we had still done things by the book, despite having limited access to the park, even less daylight, and inclement weather, we had managed to get some great evidence to corroborate the stories told locally about Devil's Backbone.

If there had been a client involved with this case, we were sure that he/she would have been pleased, but unlike the Martin case, there was no family in need. Much like with Devil's Backbone, nothing could be taken for granted with the Martin case. It would be easy to write off some of the eccentricities of the family and to dismiss many of the claims concerning the Mississippi case—but this would be a huge mistake.

As I learned at Devil's Backbone, reserving judgment about a case until after the review is a must, and I would have to make sure to scour every second of data I had captured at the home.

The Old Talbott Tavern

Though the rumbling in the master bedroom of the Martin trailer had startled me—and even caused me to approach my investigation there more seriously—past personal experiences have taught me to be prepared for almost anything when venturing into a haunted site. And I knew from previous cases that sounds in a location were often the least of my concerns. Just take the case of Talbott Tavern for instance…

Dating back to 1779, the Old Talbott Tavern in Bardstown, Kentucky, seemed a great place to soak up some history and to get in a quality ghost hunt. We had managed to get a handful of investigations under our belt at this point (including some indoor locations, thank goodness), but we felt like we were ready to tackle a place that experienced *a lot* of paranormal activity. And so we found Talbott Tavern.

Despite the fact that Talbott Tavern is extremely open about their haunting (there are links to paranormal groups who visit the place right on their website), I still thought it best to obtain permission to visit and ghost hunt there—as well as to write about our experiences there on our brandnew website. The innkeeper I spoke to was extremely nice and helpful, giving us suggestions as to which rooms had the most activity and where the hot spots were.

But he also warned us that there would be non-ghost hunting guests staying in the tavern, too, so we would have to respect their privacy. You see, in addition to having a killer dining room and on-site lounge (the Bourbon Bar), the Old Talbott Tavern has bed-and-breakfast style rooms for rent—so we would actually be staying overnight during our investigation. And thanks to the innkeeper's suggestions, Mike and I would be staying in one of their most active rooms: the General's Quarters Room.

Other hot spots pointed out for us included an upstairs ballroom/common area called the Concord Room, which is said to have a female spirit that's often seen near the chandelier and the area around the tavern's main stairs where witnesses claim to have seen and heard things associated with a spirit or ghost.

A few other B&B rooms in the tavern have stories about them, too, but they would be occupied by other guests and thereby off-limits to us. Of these rooms, the one that I wished we could visit the most was a room that infamous gunslinger Jesse James stayed in while visiting.

According to legend, he had been sleeping in this room but woke when he realized there was a man standing at the foot of his bed. Without hesitation, he drew his firearm and shot at the intruder (most likely thinking him a lawman). Much to his amazement, the intruder then vanished right before his eyes! So it seems that Jesse James is, most likely, the first person to have ever seen a ghost in Talbott Tavern—and the bullet holes from his encounter are still present today!

After speaking to the innkeeper and working out the details of our visit with Mike (unfortunately, Brandon would have to miss out on this one), we were soon on our way to Bardstown, Kentucky.

Once we arrived and had checked into our room, we decided to take a trip around the tavern to get acclimated as well as to identify all the places the innkeeper had spoken about. During this walk, we quickly found out that we would not be investigating that night until the wee hours; the Bourbon Bar was in full swing with a band playing and the volume was loud enough that any audio or video recorders that we ran would be useless. The band performance was a detail we had not learned from the innkeeper.

We knew there was a bar on the site—and that it was a Saturday night that we were visiting—but we had neglected to see if there was live music. On a positive note, the bar did close at 1 a.m., so we would have the remainder of the night to do our investigation, so all was (for the most part) okay.

Shortly before the bar closed that night, the band stopped playing. At that point, we were able to go ahead and station some audio recorders in our room and in the Concord Room—as well as take some base readings with our EMF detectors and digital thermometers. All seemed perfectly normal until the tavern cleared completely out and the night set in. With the silence came the activity ...

We were working in the Concord Room, taking readings around the chandelier and doing some EVP work, when two significant things happened in the space of ten minutes. According to locals, the reason a spirit is often seen around the chandelier is because a woman actually hanged herself from there! I had just asked an EVP question about this very legend when we heard/saw a door handle jiggle, then turn, and then the entire door swinging wide open.

This was done so matter-of-factly that neither of us thought it was paranormal until we saw there was nobody on the other side of the door. We thought that, perhaps, we had gotten too loud and disturbed a guest and that person was coming to let us know. Or that it was something else along those lines. But nobody was at the door, in the hall, or anywhere in the vicinity for that matter!

We were just digesting this event when I was suddenly blasted with the biggest, strongest cold spot that I (to this day) have ever felt. Have you ever gone into your house on a summer day and opened up your refrigerator's freezer to cool off? You know that blast of cold air that hits you when you open the freezer door? Multiply that times three and you will have some idea of what hit me.

I had just closed the hallway door that had opened and sat down in a chair when the cold spot swept across my entire back. I immediately stood and told Mike what had happened. Moving as quickly as possible, we took a temperature reading of the area and found that there was a 28-degree drop—and this was after a few moments of dissipating. Activity was clearly ramping up in the Old Talbott Tavern!

Now that we had the attention of whatever (or whoever) was with us in the B&B, we decided to do a Q&A with an EMF detector. The way this works is that we hold out the detector, which should have a flat reading, and then we ask a yes/no question. If any entity is present, and wants to answer "yes," it simply has to move toward the detector to make it light up (most investigators believe that spirits give off electromagnetic fields and, as a result, their presence will trigger an EMF detector).

After just a few questions, it was quite obvious that we were not alone. The EMF detector would go from 0 mG (milligauss) to 15 mG in the blink of an eye—but, stranger than that, the hair on my arm would actually stand up when the detector went off! It was almost like an electric charge was in the air. With several successful yes answers under our belt, I decided to try something else. Apparently I was feeling quite bold that evening.

With a grin, I asked if "anyone present" could come over and actually touch my hand. Much to my alarm, it did. Twice. The first time, the EMF detector slowly started to beep—then it got steadily faster until it lit completely up and I felt a heavy pressure actually slap against the back of my hand!

Even though I had just asked for this very thing to happen, I was not ready for it. I immediately jerked my hand away and the detector went completely flat. After a few moments of catching my breath, I steeled my will and tried again. I apologized and asked to be touched again. And it happened again. This time I tried to keep my hand in place, but it was impossible. As soon as there was contact, I jerked my hand back again. It was almost like an involuntary reaction.

I apologized, and we went back to doing more EVP work. Once we were finished with the Concord Room, it was almost 5 a.m., so we told the room that we were retiring to our quarters for the night, but anyone there was welcome to join us. Much to our surprise, we would not be retiring alone…

After settling into our beds for the night (the General's Quarters has two twin beds, thankfully), Mike and I were chatting across the room to each other. We had placed several audio recorders in the bedroom for the night and we had an EMF detector set up on a small nightstand between the two beds. This would serve as an alarm of sorts; if any entity was present, and it approached the beds, theoretically the detector would start beeping and lighting up.

Joking, I asked Mike, "If that thing starts beeping in the night, is it going to wake you up?" He laughed, saying, "Oh, hell yeah. You'll probably have to do a double take to find me because I'll probably be hanging from the canopy." He was referring to the lace cloth that draped the tops of the canopy beds.

I laughed, but he suddenly got quiet and said, "I just felt a cool breeze that went across my face!" I got up and took the EMF detector over to the bed. Nothing. We laughed again and quickly went back to bed—and it wasn't long before we were asleep.

Interestingly, the audio from the room would reveal why Mike felt that cool breeze…When I listened to our conversation about the EMF detector a couple days later, there was a third voice in the room with us! Right after Mike said I'd have to do a double take to find him, a strange male voice answered with a quick guttural laugh! Then you hear Mike say he felt the cold breeze.

This audio clip, along with the personal experiences we had while we there, make the Old Talbott Tavern one of our most memorable ghost hunts. And I learned a few valuable lessons during the trip, too:

1. Even though you think you are ready for an otherworldly encounter, you're probably not. There really is no way to prepare for such a thing.

2. As long as you remain relatively calm, you can overcome fear. You may get startled, you may even get frightened, but take a deep breath and remain calm. If necessary, calmly leave the area. Just don't panic.

3. You can have some of the best personal experiences ever and still leave with very little actual evidence. During the heat of battle in the Concord Room, we had neglected to turn on our camcorder to record the events. We got it all on audio, but the video would have been much better in this circumstance. So after all that had happened, all we really left the tavern with as evidence was the EVP captured in our bedroom.

Regardless, it was a great trip and an even better investigation. We left the tavern ready for more. I would have to apply this enthusiasm to my ongoing investigation of the Martin home.

Though I had already experienced a few things in the trailer—specifically the loud rumble and the shadowy figure—the potential for more startling events was ever present. There was no way to know for certain whether Tim had actually experienced possession while living in the home, but it was quite obvious that at least one spirit present could actually touch people and move objects. Thankfully, my time at Talbott Tavern prepared me for just such instances.

Magnolia Manor

After spending an evening in the Martin home, one thing was certain: I would be going back. Having personal experiences during one short investigation is a rare occurrence—and is usually a sure sign that ongoing paranormal activity is most likely happening. Because of this, I knew that I would be making several more trips into the Mississippi delta in the near future (a thought that drew a sigh of resignation from me as I drove back to Tennessee).

Over the years since we first decided to relocate and base our group out of Memphis, Tennessee, we have spent a lot of time at a number of local haunted places. And this is a good thing. One thing we have learned during our investigations is that maintaining a good relationship with clients is essential if you plan to have a good, local reputation—and if you want to make a second trip there.

In addition to this, there are some places that we just plain love! Such is the case with the haunted bed-and-breakfast in Bolivar, Tennessee, that's known as Magnolia Manor. Besides being honest about their haunting, the owners actually host haunted tours in the fall (leading up to Halloween), and welcome ghost enthusiasts who want to rent a room in the B&B.

We have had the pleasure of investigating this wonderful and historic antebellum home many times—and it is easily one of the most active haunted places we have ever been to. In fact, we have stayed in the home (as well as the small cottage out back) more than ten times and we have *always* come away with great evidence—and, on occasion, significant personal experiences.

Magnolia Manor, in its own way, has also been a sort of school for learning about the paranormal for us. Since we now know the place so well—and have learned to even recognize certain ghostly voices via EVP—we have been able to do far more experimenting here than at any other location. Typically, if we want to try a new investigative technique, we go to Magnolia Manor. Why? Because if we don't get a reaction there, we probably won't anywhere!

It was through our investigations at this home that we also formed and developed "DICE," our basic method for conducting an investigation. DICE stands for "Detect, Interact, Capture, and Escalate," and it is the foundation for everything we do. It's just one more reason why we love this location.

Magnolia Manor was built by Judge Austin Miller in 1849 and it served as the Miller family home until the 1970s. And though Judge Miller is, himself, quite a famous person in his own right, the home is mostly known for four other important people: Generals Grant, Sherman, McPherson, and Logan.

Prior to the battle of Shiloh, the Union generals stayed in the home despite the misgivings that Mrs. Miller may have had at the time (members of her immediate family were in the Confederate Army). It's thought that they may have even planned the Battle of Shiloh/Pittsburg Landing from there. But, unfortunately, the ghosts at the home are none of these men. More than likely they are members of the Miller family who passed away on the premises over the years.

Visitors who have stayed at the home have reported seeing spirits that match the descriptions of Lizzie Lea Miller and Annie Miller—and they are most likely not alone, since a male spirit has also been documented there, too!

Guests who stay at the B&B have four rooms to choose from—and we have had experiences in all of them—as well as the cottage behind the house. Here are a few of our more dramatic moments in this house (and what we learned from them)...

Our first big experience happened while we were shooting a segment of a documentary called *Ghosts of War* in the house. We were filming in a room called the C. A. Miller Suite next to a rocking chair that's said to often have a spectral woman sitting in it. I was asking some EVP questions and attempting to get the woman to appear for us. Of course, this was not happening.

Mike then suggested that I actually sit in the chair, thinking this might provoke the spirit into appearing, since I would be sitting in "her chair." So we pointed our cameras at the chair and I did just that. No sooner did I sit down that I noticed a pale, wispy figure beginning to appear in the far corner of the room. It actually looked like the upper torso, one arm, and the bald head of a man!

I immediately leaped from the chair and began pointing at the figure. The cameras spun around, but it was already gone. Just like that. But the story doesn't end there. Because we were also doing an investigation (not just shooting a movie), we had audio recorders running in the room.

Right after I had seen the partial apparition, we were discussing moving the cameras once again so that we could get in frame the area that the apparition had appeared in. When we reviewed our audio recorder from that moment, there was an interesting EVP. Immediately after it is suggested that we move the camera, a strange male voice says, "Put that sucker over there!"

The entity was actually toying with us! And, possibly, even avoiding us to an extent. That simple EVP taught us that, try as you might, you can investigate in the most haunted of places and still possibly walk away with nothing.

Why? Because if the spirits are intelligent, they may actually be avoiding you. This also teaches us that just because nothing paranormal is happening at a particular place during your investigation, something could very well be happening somewhere else.

Another significant moment we had in Magnolia Manor happened in what is known as the 1849 Room. It had already been an active night with several small occurrences, so we had migrated into this room to take a break. As Mike and I sat in the room and talked, it became apparent that we were not alone.

At one point, both of us stopped talking because the crystal clear sound of a woman laughing was coming from just outside the bedroom door! I quickly got up, went to the door, and opened it. Nothing. Nobody in sight. So I closed the door and returned to the bed. A few moments later, the same thing—only louder and more sustained. Again, I got up and checked the hallway. Nobody was there. In fact, the only female in the entire place was the owner, and she had already turned in for the night downstairs.

Later, when we reviewed all of our audio and video recorders in the house, the disembodied laughs were recorded on a whopping three devices. Not only were the sounds loud enough for us to hear in real time, but they were of a volume significant enough to be recorded two rooms away. That's a heckuva disembodied voice.

So what did this teach us? A strange but true lesson: sometimes the best way to get a spirit to pay attention to you is to ignore it. Though we'd had some activity at Magnolia Manor earlier that evening, it wasn't until we stopped and did our own thing that the spirit felt compelled to do something dramatic—almost like a child who has been ignored. As strange as that sounds, it worked at this location and has worked many times since.

The final incident I want to mention at this home involves the cottage that's out back, behind the house. Today that area is a self-contained mini-house that visitors can rent and stay in. But in past years, it was the servants' quarters. Over the years, various paranormal groups have stayed in the cottage and gotten some great EVPs. So, knowing this, we spent a lot of time in the cottage attempting to do the same thing.

Since we had already heard evidence caught by other groups from the cottage, we were able to skip the preliminaries and go straight to asking questions directly to the spirit that we had heard recorded by others. This saved a lot of time and got us some great interaction with the spirit. Once we started hearing some odd sounds coming from the little kitchen in the cottage (Mike and I were sitting in the living room for the EVP session), we decided to implement a technique called Singapore Theory.

Basically, Singapore Theory involves playing music from the era that you think a ghost once lived in. It's thought that this might entice a spirit to participate with investigators— or at least come in to check out the music! We started by playing old songs that would have been around in the late 1800s—mostly Civil War-era songs. Nothing happened.

After a few tunes, we moved forward to some circa 1920s jazz and big band tunes. This hit the mark. Not long after the first song started, noises in the kitchen started getting louder. At one point, it actually sounded like a heavy person suddenly stepped on the metal furnace that was in the floor directly behind us. Now that we knew we had the attention of whoever was there, we started trading songs for activity.

In other words, we would turn off the music, ask if we should play another song, then ask for a tap or knock response. When we managed to get those, we then started asking for the entity to speak to us. A review of the audio we captured in the cottage that night was amazing. Not only were we getting the knocks and taps we requested, but a mysterious male voice (possibly a young boy) was actually imitating us.

Several times over the course of the investigation, I would say something and, immediately after I said it, the strange voice would try to repeat what I just said. And the voice had an eerie quality to it—like it was spoken through a mouth full of food or something. At one point, the spirit even said Mike's name.

We learned that night that experimenting with new techniques like Singapore Theory is a must—and that we can't give up on something just because it isn't immediately working. The spirit didn't want to communicate with us initially, but once we found the right combination of requests and songs, we got more than we bargained for.

Another point worth noting is that investigators should always pay attention to what is reported at a location. It would have been easy to blow off the reports of other paranormal groups (or even the residents there), but paying attention to their information, as well the hot spots pointed out to us, allowed us to spend our time concentrating on things that would be successful, rather than fumbling to do something/anything randomly that may or may not work.

Looking back at cases like Magnolia Manor, the Old Talbott Tavern, and even way back to Devil's Backbone, one thing is crystal clear: we must never stop learning! There is no single way to perform an investigation. While we at Paranormal Inc will always approach a case scientifically, there are many ways to do this—and, I'm sure, many ways that have yet to be discovered.

I only hoped that my past experiences and methods that I learned from cases like these would help me out with the Martin family. After one evening in the trailer, I was already experiencing some new occurrences, so I just hoped that I would find the right combination of techniques and approach to bring about some resolution for everyone there.

Much like with Magnolia Manor, I would have to pay attention to the hot spots of the Martin home and not be afraid to try some new techniques and to experiment. Also, I would have to pay attention to any evidence that I managed to capture during my first visit. Of course, I would have to finish the long drive back home before I could review anything I had captured during my first investigation...

5

EXAMINING THE DATA

It was now time to go over the massive amount of photographic, audio, and video evidence that I had collected during my night at the Martin residence. This is the work that separates the recreational ghost hunters from true paranormal investigators. Over the course of my six hours in the home, I had used two camcorders, three audio recorders, and a still camera in almost constant operation.

This meant I had over 300 photographs to review, 18 hours of audio to listen to, and 12 hours of video to watch. And this didn't include the DVR system (with multiple camera angles) and audio recorders that the Mississippi group had rolling during the evening. My only consolation was that they would be reviewing that footage.

With a recreational ghost hunt, like those listed on the Paranormal Inc website, our team may take up to several weeks to go through this much data. This is because there is no immediate need to assist anyone. (Recreational ghost hunts usually take place at museums, bed-and-breakfasts, etc., that typically just like having evidence of their haunting for publicity or for personal satisfaction.)

But with a case that involves a private residence and actual, concerned residents, an effort has to be made to wrap up a review as quickly as possible. Joanne and her family would be sitting on pins and needles until we informed her one way or the other about what we did or didn't find during our visit. And who could blame her?

After informing my wife that I would be locked away in "the cave" for many hours (possibly days) doing a review, I settled in with my headphones and fired up the computer. Thanks to today's technology, the information gathered at a typical ghost hunt can be scrutinized with a fine-toothed comb without ever leaving the comfort of your home workstation.

Photos would be dissected and analyzed with Adobe Photoshop, audio with Audacity and Soundforge, and video with Sony Vegas (my nonlinear editing program of choice). Even the notes taken during the investigation could be transcribed and saved in a Microsoft Word document for archival purposes.

Performing a review in this manner is great because it's straightforward, allows for easy archiving, and makes sending a copy of the entire data (including notes, findings, etc.)

to the owner of a property as easy as burning a DVD-ROM or just emailing the files.

With all the footage now lit up in front of me on my monitor, I took a deep breath and waded in with more than a mild expectation of finding something extraordinary. I started with the photographs. I carefully scanned each photo taken for anything that appeared to be out of place.

Beginning with the upper-left corner of each photo, I would slowly pan in a clockwise circle around the image, slowly working my way toward the center. This allows me to check every pixel for anything untoward.

Looking at some of the rooms for the second time, I was still amazed by the level of sheer mess that lay about the place. Fortunately, though, mess is not paranormal! Nothing immediately jumped out at me as I reviewed the photos. In the end, though I had taken numerous photographs, only one seemed to contain something of an odd nature.

I had taken a series of photographs outside the front of the trailer using the "night shot" feature of my Sony still camera. The perk of using this feature is that you need little to no light to get a great shot—and you also capture a portion of the light spectrum that is usually not visible to the human eye (infrared). Many investigators believe that the energy needed to facilitate a haunting—and possibly even an actual ghost—can be visible in the infrared spectrum.

In this case, I had snapped a photo of the trailer's front window, where the television had made its impromptu exit, and then I took a step to my right and had taken a second photo of the same area by the front steps. The first photo contained nothing. The second, however, appeared to have a strange bearded face peering from beside the steps. I zoomed in on the photograph and took a closer look. It definitely appeared to be someone, or something.

Of course, I have been fooled by such photos in the past. When human eyes look at a picture that contains little to no obvious features, the mind tries to form recognizable images from that nothingness. This is called "matrixing."

Looking at the photo in front of me, my mind was now matrixing a strange, bearded fellow. Or not. It was entirely possible that this was a photo of something paranormal. I suddenly wondered what John or Keith looked like—though this looked more like an aborigine from Australia than an American male living in Mississippi.

For comparison, I pulled up the reference photos that I had taken of the trailer to see if I could discern what the face could possibly be. Though I had not taken a second photo from the same exact angle, I had plenty of shots of the front of the trailer. I found nothing that would explain the face.

I would have to send the photograph to the folks in Mississippi for a second opinion and give them the chance to debunk the photo. Often, returning to the site of a photograph can assist with this. I cautioned Terri and Patricia, though, to keep the photograph to themselves. If Joanne saw the photograph, no amount of debunking, explaining, or reassuring would keep her from believing that this was, indeed, a photo of one of her ghosts. Setting the photo aside for the moment, I moved on to review the video I had captured.

Reviewing the video from the Martin investigation was like watching the world's most boring reality television show: people would occasionally shuffle in front of the camera and say something, dust would fly by, and objects that were in frame simply refused to move of their accord. Damn them!

I watched the recordings very carefully—mostly because I did not want to have to watch them a second time—and saw/heard nothing out of the ordinary. Twelve hours and 200 yawns later, I wrapped up this part of the review with nothing to show for it. Unfortunately, this is usually the case with video.

As I've learned from years of experience, pointing a camcorder at the right place—and at the right time—can be a difficult chore at best (remember the apparition at Magnolia Manor?). I had to hope that the DVR system the Mississippi team had in place had managed to capture something paranormal (and hopefully the materialization of the watch in the master bedroom). Now it was time to move on to the audio recordings—typically the most fruitful footage collected during an investigation.

Unlike the photos and video, going over the audio would prove to be the most challenging—and the most rewarding—part of the review. The challenge came from the fact that there were eight people present in the small trailer—and it was rare that all eight of us stopped talking at the same time.

Of course, through most of the recordings, only the folks doing EVP (electronic voice phenomena) work were speaking, with the rest of us sitting quietly and listening for any type of response. There were also huge chunks of audio where nobody was in the room at all with the audio recorder, so reviewing this audio was quite easy.

Once I became accustomed to the voices of those who were present, and I was able to consult my notes to see where everyone was located at what time, analyzing the audio became a (relatively) straightforward task.

Over the course of reviewing the eighteen hours of audio, I found several different, but interesting, clips:

1. When I was initially in the master bedroom doing some EVP work with Terri, the audio recorder captured a strange voice that sounded exactly like a young girl—and there were no young girls present in the place. And, strangely enough, it almost sounded like the girl said "mommy" when Joanne was speaking in the adjoining living room. Emily perhaps?

2. Again, I was performing EVP work in the master bedroom when the audio recorder captured the crystal clear sounds of a young girl speaking (again) in the background. Several syllables are audible, though I could not recognize any specific words.

3. Right after the second recording of the young girl speaking, I asked another couple of EVP questions

and then there's the infamous rumble in the master bedroom. It was loud and clear on the audio recorder, just as I suspected. It's always nice when evidence backs up a personal experience!

4. A little while later, after the same audio recorder captured the rumble, a couple members of the Mississippi group were performing EVP work with me again in the master bedroom. I ask for anybody "present" to knock on the wall for me. There is a clear knock of response that we heard while listening to the recording in real time (which verified what I had heard on location, though I wasn't absolutely certain).

5. At one point, we were all outside taking a break, so the trailer was completely empty. An audio recorder in the master bedroom had managed to record an audible male moan and the sound of a bang—almost as if someone was trying to get our attention. Was this another case of an entity not liking being ignored? I would have to explore this during my next visit.

6. The audio recorder that was placed in Julie's bedroom picked up several interesting things. Several times over the course of the evening, a clear voice whispering could be heard in the room. During these occasions, you can hear us working in the background in another room—and most of the time, this room is sealed off from the rest of

the trailer, so you can only hear a muffled version of our voices (and this is only when we are talking at full volume). So for a whisper to be so clear and audible, it would have had to occur right by the recorder. On another interesting note, at times the whispers sounded male and at others, female.

Now I was really scratching my head. The evidence seemed to indicate that something, indeed, was afoot at the Martin home. Most of the activity had happened in the master bedroom—just like Joanne and the others said. And there seemed to be at least one male and one female entity in the trailer—also, just like they had reported. And while at no point did any voice confirm a name for any of the entities, the benefit of the doubt now had to swing in favor of Joanne and family.

Once I had documented all the things I had found during my review, I made a quick call to the Mississippi group to let them know what I had found and to check in with their review. Unfortunately, nothing untoward was found on their audio and video equipment.

The video camera that was placed in the master bedroom was, unfortunately, out of frame when the watch materialized, so there was no footage to back this up. This, of course, was crushing news to me. I had hoped that this had been captured on video, as it would have made for some rather dramatic evidence.

Terri then reiterated to me Joanne's desire to have the house blessed, so I agreed to find someone to do this before I returned. Since I had captured some relatively good evidence of the haunting, returning to the trailer to discuss the findings with Joanne would be necessary. It would also give me the opportunity to perform a follow-up investigation and possibly debunk the photo I had taken personally.

In a lot of ways, I dreaded returning to Mississippi and telling Joanne and her family about my findings. While I was sure that they would be relieved to get some confirmation of paranormal activity, I was also sure that this might make them even more anxious about staying in the trailer over the long term.

But, even worse, there was the possibility that playing the EVP voices could cause them to spiral even further into their obsession concerning the activity and cause even more paranoia/hysteria. It was to be a dreaded meeting, indeed…

The Nonreality of Reality Television

Most associate sitting down with the owners of a haunted place to discuss the evidence found during an investigation with the television show *Ghost Hunters*. On this program, the members of TAPS (The Atlantic Paranormal Society) sit pleasantly across from the owners of the property they have just investigated, and then show them what they have found, and everyone leaves with a joke and a smile.

Of course, there is also a camera rolling the entire time, so it's no wonder the property owners always seem a little too comfortable with the findings—even findings that contradict their own experiences.

In real life, this is not always the case. In fact, it usually *isn't* the case. If you bring back evidence of a haunting to an owner who wants nothing to do with such a thing (or is possibly frightened by it), there is usually a great deal of panic that must be dealt with. What do they do about the haunting? Should they call in a priest?

Conversely, sometimes clients really want their home or business to be haunted for whatever reason—or they are completely convinced that they have a ghost. Telling these people that you found nothing can open a whole can of indignation and finger-pointing regarding your investigation methods. In these instances, it's usually best to point out that spirits don't perform on cue and that finding no evidence doesn't necessarily mean a place isn't haunted. Then run.

It's actually quite amazing how many investigators in the field have learned how to ghost hunt from watching television programs. They're pretty easy to spot—especially when you take them out with you on an investigation. They will typically have unusually low attention spans, use terms like "dead time," and tend to gravitate toward trendy gear like the ridiculously ludicrous "Frank's Box" or "Radio Shack Hack" (essentially an AM/FM radio with a broken scan button that can supposedly tune in the voices of the dead).

On the positive side, the ghost programs have done a few good things for the paranormal field. The popularity of such things as EMF detectors and infrared illuminators have caused the prices of these items to drop considerably, since more of these types of products are sold these days—and the availability of these devices is at an all-time high.

It's also much more acceptable to admit you actually work in the paranormal field, you are a ghost hunting enthusiast, or that you have a haunting. Of course this openness has also created a whole new marketing strategy for a number of places (the haunted tourist stop) and created rock stars out of certain televised paranormal groups, but you take the good with the bad, right?

That said, I doubted that the "reveal" at the Martin trailer would be anything like the shows on television.

Making a Few Calls

The evidence we gathered during our first night at the trailer, coupled with some of our personal experiences, seemed to confirm that the place was haunted. Whether or not any of the entities could be considered "nonhuman," though, was still up in the air. I had found nothing that would support this (and I couldn't seriously consider the moth)—though if I were to take the possessions seriously, this type of event would be more likely to occur with such a presence in the trailer. I decided this would be a good question to ask some clergy.

Not surprisingly, as soon as I started contacting various churches in Joanne's area, it became clear that nobody was interested in visiting the trailer. The home was square in the middle of Baptist/Pentecostal country, and the idea of blessing a haunted trailer was simply a nonstarter.

I kept searching, though, and while looking on the internet I came across an interesting blog that was written by a Catholic priest named Father Joe Jenkins (his real name), who is the pastor of the Holy Family Church and a priest in the Archdiocese of Washington, DC.

Father Joe had written an article about the infamous possession case portrayed in the movie *The Exorcist* and seemed quite knowledgeable on the subject. Furthermore, he actually knew one of the priests involved with that case. After reading his articles on possession, I decided to contact him for some advice concerning the episodes involving Tim, even though I knew I might not get a reply from him before heading back to Mississippi (or at all).

In the meantime, my search for a home blessing had paid off. I received an email from a minister I'll call "Frank" who serviced a Unitarian church in Alabama. He was open to the possibility of hauntings and ghosts and was more than willing to visit Joanne's home to bless it. I thanked him (and my lucky stars) and decided to make another call: to the sheriff's office where Joanne lived.

After much explaining to the amusement of the deputy on call at the sheriff's office, I managed to get a few pieces of information about the Martin home and family:

1. The trailer was known locally for being haunted. According to this deputy, stories about the ghosts there were spread by local kids who heard first-hand tales from (probably) Julie. As a result, not *all* the rocks and the like thrown at the trailer were done by invisible hands.

2. Officers had, indeed, responded to several calls at the residence—including a night where two squad cars were sitting in Joanne's driveway getting bombarded by rocks that came from nowhere. The angry officers quickly scouted the area, flashlights in hand, looking for the perpetrators, but could find no one. They even called out a fire unit that brought along a thermal camera, hoping to see the heat signature of someone hiding in the trees. But nobody was there and the rocks still came.

3. The officer also confirmed the area's history of racial violence. In the not-too-distant past, quite a few people had turned up missing or dead there. As he asked me more about this subject, I realized I had gotten very few specifics concerning "John" or what may have happened to him. I resolved to correct this when I returned to the trailer.

Not long after getting this information, I received an email from Father Joe Jenkins, the priest I had contacted. He told me some interesting things...

The Exorcist

Whether or not most people know it, the case of possession that's portrayed in the movie *The Exorcist* is a true one. Only it didn't involve a young girl. The real victim was a young boy who lived in Cottage City, Maryland. Author Peter Blatty read about the case in the local paper there and then went on to write his best-selling book about the subject.

More recently, author Thomas B. Allen penned a book titled *Possessed* that details the actual events surrounding the real exorcism of the boy from Maryland. Though this book is, in itself, quite riveting reading, I picked up a copy for an entirely different reason.

Though I was interested in reading the book, I was mostly intrigued by the "diary" that was kept by the performers of the original exorcism during their ritual. This diary is included in the back of the book *Possessed* for everyone to read. And riveting stuff it is.

According to the book, after the boy consulted with a local priest in Mt. Rainier, Maryland, concerning the strange things that were happening to him, he actually traveled with his mother to St. Louis, Missouri, to undergo the ritual of exorcism. During this ceremony, the Jesuit priests involved (Fathers Bishop, Bowdern, and Halloran) documented what happened in the diary. I was curious how many of the documented "symptoms" of possession, as well as personal experiences that occurred during the exorcism, would apply to Tim and his episodes.

Interestingly, there were a few parallel events. Specifically, the young boy was initially plagued by the sounds of scratching in the floor/walls of his bedroom and objects that seemed to move around him of their own accord. Both of these things had happened in the Martin home—with Tim present in the living room.

When the clergy looked into the background of the boy's household, there was evidence that an aunt who was into Spiritualism had used a Ouija board on the premises, and also possibly held a séance. These were elements that, to my knowledge, did not occur in the Martin property, though I would specifically find out on my return visit.

Also, the boy would go on to experience his bed vibrating/banging and priests attending the boy would witness pieces of heavy furniture moving by themselves. Again, this was just a little *too* close to the furniture/bed flying about the master bedroom at the Martin trailer for my taste. But that was where the comparisons stopped, since Tim had never remained for any length of time in a possessed state.

Father Joe Jenkins had mentioned much of this information on his website, as well as debunked many of the myths that now surround the famous possession case (mostly due to the sensational nature of the movie). Luckily, the priest had found the time to respond to the email I had sent him regarding the Martin case and the possible possession there.

In his email to me, he wrote that, "Various elements you describe are familiar," in reference to the events surrounding

Tim's bouts of possession, and then he related to me something that I did not know.

According to Gabriele Amorth, the chief exorcist to the diocese of Rome, most (if not all) hauntings have a demonic element to them. He states that these demons delight in mimicking the dead and that the more the family dwells/ obsesses on the ghost/demon, the more power it has. Gulp.

I had also asked the priest in my email whether or not he believed in the famous exorcism case portrayed in the movie/book, and whether he thought the boy was, indeed, actually possessed, as many have claimed. Not only did Father Joe think the boy was possessed, but he personally knew a priest in Maryland who was involved with the case and who was forever changed by what he had witnessed from the boy.

While I was digesting all of this information, a strange thought suddenly struck me. Didn't the movie *The Exorcist II: The Heretic* have a moth in it? I took a trip to my local movie store, bought the movie, and gave it a watch— and, sure enough, the demon in the movie would often fly around as an insect (I couldn't tell if it was a moth or not, but it sure looked like one).

Could the exorcist movies be influencing Tim and Joanne's opinion of their haunting? If they were, this wouldn't be a first. As I previously mentioned, rectories all over the country were flooded with false possession cases when the original movie was screened.

It was obvious that this case wasn't getting any easier. As amazing as the eyewitness accounts were with the Martin case, it was clear that I would have to be open to the possibility that they could be experiencing exactly what they claimed.

Planning a Second Trip

Armed with all this new information and having arranged for a blessing of the home, I felt like I could now return to the Martin household. Despite the opinion of Father Amorth, I still decided to avoid any reference to possession, exorcism, or infestation regarding this case.

I feared that if the investigation spiraled down this path, things could go very bad, very fast. I was barely able to arrange a house blessing, so I didn't want to imagine the difficulty involved with getting a Catholic priest to the home to investigate the possible need for an exorcism (if the ritual could even be done for a non-Catholic).

I was convinced a blessing would put the Martin family's minds at ease and that despite the evidence I had gotten, they could come to terms with the idea of ghost or two residing on their property.

Unfortunately, it would take a few weeks to make the return voyage into the delta and a few things would change in the Martin household. It was also at this time that I started experiencing some strange activity myself...

6

TROUBLE AT HOME

As I mentioned earlier, I once lived in a house with a mild haunting. And though the ghost there did little to indicate its presence, I always lived with the knowledge that it was, indeed, there.

Over the years, though, I slowly became accustomed to my unseen guest—especially when I looked at the whole situation as a mystery that needed to be solved. But, unfortunately, having a ghost wasn't the only unexplainable thing to happen to me while living in this house.

In addition to having a resident spirit in my bedroom, two other events took place while I lived in Scott City, Missouri, that could be labeled as being paranormal. The first of these happened to be a recurring incident that investigators over the years have dubbed "getting hagged."

Since ancient times, people have reported experiencing the feeling of waking up from their sleep during the night and being unable to move. In many countries, this condition is called "Old Hag Syndrome." This is due to traditional folklore that tells of an old woman who would visit people during the night and sit upon their chest as they slept. According to these stories, this old woman was typically a demon who would use this opportunity to leech the life from her victims. It is this very legend that has spawned such creatures as succubae, incubi, and vampires. And it is the Old Hag who is said to ride her victims much like a "night mare"—a term that is still used today to describe a particularly nasty dream.

Prior to living in the haunted house in Scott City, I had never experienced this condition. But not long after moving in, I started being hagged on a regular basis—about once every other week.

It is a horrible affair—especially to children. I remember waking up, being unable to move, but aware of everything going on around me. I could hear the silence of the room (itself a powerful and heavy thing), feel the bed beneath me, and even smell familiar scents. But I could not move at all. This would have been bad enough, but the attack did not end with just that. Oh, no. There was more.

In addition to being paralyzed, there was also the overwhelming sensation of a presence being in the room with me. It did not specifically feel as if something was sitting on me, as the legend suggests, but in my mind I knew there was something in my bedroom with me. And it wasn't pleasant.

What's more, I could sense that it was moving, approaching the bed. This was when things got terrifying. I would try to cry out, but my voice would not cooperate. Eventually, if I was scared enough or the presence got too close, I would suddenly snap out of the ordeal. I would wake up with a jerk and sit up in the bed in a cold sweat.

After experiencing this very event many times, I soon began to dread going to sleep. It was bad enough that the closet door would eventually open by itself, but now I had to worry about some mysterious entity that paralyzed me in my bed at night! Back then I did not have the information that I have now about hagging; all I knew was that my room was a hall of terror when the lights went out.

These days, scientists have correlated Old Hag Syndrome with a medical condition called "sleep paralysis," but paranormal investigators have learned (including me) that people who live in haunted locations seem particularly afflicted by this malady. Could it be that this sensation is not always a simple medical condition? Maybe there's a little bit more to do with this syndrome than meets the eye— something that gives a bit of credence to all the old tales. Something that science simply cannot explain away.

When my family moved from the haunted place in Scott City, I never had another hagging incident. Not once in the remainder of my childhood. Not once in my adult life. That is to say, I *didn't* have any further haggings until I visited the Martin place …

Nightmares, Etc.

While I was involved with and investigating the Martin case, I was also experiencing a few life changes of my own. I had recently moved into my first house (that I owned) along with my wife, and now we were going to have our first child.

So, needless to say, reviewing all the evidence from my investigation, as well as coordinating my visits to Mississippi, was being juggled with all the mundane logistics involved with maintaining a new place and preparing for a baby. Somehow, I managed to get through all of this—but not without experiencing some strange evenings in the new house.

Not long after finishing my review of all the footage captured during my first visit and planning the details of my second visit to the Martin home, I woke one night to an all-too-familiar sensation. It was a hagging—though slightly different from those I had experienced as a young man. I still could not move, and I was still aware of everything in the room (such as my wife lying beside me), but there was no fear. There also didn't seem to be anything in the room with me. Or at least I didn't sense anything.

When the event was over, I simply sat up, shook off the heebie-jeebies, and took a long look around the empty room. Maybe it was a product of being "all grown up," but it wasn't quite the horrible experience that I remembered having as a child. But this wouldn't be the end of it.

This experience happened a couple of times and eventually culminated in one strange evening. On this particular night, I had a relatively nasty nightmare. I can't remember the specifics, but it had something to do with an intruder in my house. I have a nightly habit of personally checking every door (wherever I am) before I go to sleep, so I can remember thinking in my sleep, "I know I locked all the doors. How did someone get in?"

The dream must not have lasted long, though, because I woke up not long after falling asleep, once again, to the strange feeling of paralysis. But this time, by sheer willpower, I snapped almost instantly out of it, jerking up in the bed. Now, believe it or not, here's the weird part...

For a moment, when I first woke up, I could have sworn that I saw the silhouette of a short person (perhaps a child) standing beside my side of the bed. I instantly jerked away from the figure, which woke my sleeping wife. She asked what was wrong, I mumbled something about a bad dream, and she immediately dozed off to sleep again. Sleep took a bit longer for me, however.

Why was I suddenly experiencing these things again? I was relatively sure I hadn't moved into a new haunted place, so I assumed I was simply having nightmares because of being in a new house, the combined stress of moving, and expecting a baby. And, certainly, the evidence I had captured at the Martin trailer was weighing on me (as well as the prospect of returning there to explain it all to Joanne).

But I had no reason to believe that a ghost, or anything else paranormal for that matter, had followed me home. Though many investigators believe that spirits can follow a living person to a new place, I could not imagine any spirit wanting to follow me home (though my wife has always jokingly warned me to not bring home ghosts from the cases I investigate). And I certainly didn't feel like I was obsessing over the subject of ghosts or demons.

It was all quite perplexing and before long I began to question whether or not I had actually seen a figure by the bed. "Maybe I was still asleep and dreaming somehow," I would tell myself. But I knew otherwise.

Experience has taught me that when a person has something unexplainable and/or terrifying happen to them, that person's mind will immediately begin to doubt what was witnessed. Sometimes within hours, a person will even recant their own eyewitness account and write it all off as a mistake or imagination at work.

During the interviews at the Martin trailer, Tim (aka Hot Boy) had said something about one of the entities there that had stuck with me. "It won't let you sleep," he said. "It constantly messes with you, messes with your head."

In the end, I decided to chalk up the whole affair as a product of me delving into the Martin case too intently and working far too many hours. Since I was re-experiencing a paranormal event from my past, though, I began to wonder if another type of activity would start to reoccur as well…

Corner Demons

As I mentioned above, there were two additional, strange things that happened while I was living in the haunted home in Scott City, Missouri. The second concerns the subject of "corner demons."

I don't remember where I first heard the term—though I believe it was actually at a church I went to with a friend (a Church of God or Church of Christ, I do believe). The gist of it is this: supposedly, every single person who walks the Earth has a guardian angel and a demon that is assigned to watch over them, and these beings have the ability to influence our decisions on a daily basis.

According to the spinner of this yarn, it is said that we can, on occasion, actually catch a glimpse of one of these entities—though to look directly at it would mean instant madness. I, of course, queried how this was possible. I was given this example:

Have you ever been watching television or reading a book and you thought you saw something move out of the corner of your eye? That was one of your assignees. It simply stopped moving for a moment and you noticed it. Because of this apparent ability to see these creatures out of the corner of our eye, they are simply called corner demons (since nobody is particularly afraid of angels, the story deals mainly with the demon side of things).

According to the same tale, if you were to accidentally see one of these so-called corner demons straight on (especially if you saw or looked right into its face), you would go insane from fright.

I was immediately intrigued by all this information, though nobody I knew had ever heard of such a thing. This was because I often saw dark shapes out of the corner of my eyes while I lived in the old, haunted house. And after hearing the story, I always wondered if, someday, I would accidentally find myself staring face to face with some demonic entity.

Over the years since I first heard this story, I've never managed to find anything else out about corner demons. For all I know, this was just a spooky yarn made up by the preacher at that particular church.

Today, seeing dark shapes out of the corner of your eye or anywhere else (sometimes in the shape of an actual person) is a common paranormal experience—especially in haunted locations. Sometimes they are called shadow people or black masses, but investigators tend to have a great deal of disagreement concerning the nature of these beings. Are they evil? Or are they simply another form a spirit can take on after death?

Since I have little faith in the existence of demons, I have always chosen to believe that these dark entities are just another type of ghost—the spirit of someone who has passed on from this life. Or it's a bug or some other common thing that we are all glimpsing out of the corner of our eye! I certainly do not think all these things we are seeing are demons or the Devil.

But, as mentioned before, it does not mean that I'm not afraid of the Devil. Like most who have grown up in a Christian household, I have a particular fear of just such a being. And I definitely do not want to have any kind of run-in with such a thing. This is mostly for the obvious reasons, but this is also because I have had a personal experience concerning the Devil in the past.

A Sad Tale of Warning

As with the Martin family and other people mentioned in this book, I will keep the names associated with the story I'm about to tell anonymous. The details of the sordid tale I will tell here, though, are entirely and verifiably true—much to my everlasting dismay.

This story takes place when I was nineteen years old and dating a local girl in Scott City I'll call "Tara." She was much like any other American teenage girl, but her sister—I'll call her "Sarah"—was someone altogether different. Tara still lived at home along with her family, but Sarah was living on her own in a mobile home with her young daughter "Tiffany."

Since the father of Tiffany was in prison (no lie), it was just Sarah living alone in the trailer with the baby. For most folks, this would pose no problem, but Sarah was not most folks.

First of all, Sarah was quite popular with the local male population—even while she was married. Second of all, she liked to party—often and hard. And while she did take care of her baby, all of us who knew Sarah still had to wonder why she tended to get drunk so much around her child. Of course, being nineteen and unable to legally drink myself, Sarah's trailer was a sort of illicit wonderland for Tara and me.

On many a night, Tara and I would hang out at Sarah's trailer to party with the older folks, and then I would walk Tara home to make sure she was there by her curfew. On the particular night of this story, we had done just this, but unlike other nights, I would return to the trailer to sleep until morning. This was because I was planning to meet a friend there early in the morning to go to a job interview with me. (We were both attempting to get employment at the same place). And it was easier to just crash there than it was to go home.

After I had walked Tara home, I returned to the trailer to find the aftermath of a party that had clearly gone to sky-high proportions. Amidst the beer bottles, half-eaten bags of chips, and cigarette butts lying around the place, Sarah sat in a drunken heap on the floor beside a small bassinet that contained baby Tiffany.

I told Sarah that I was going to get some sleep for my interview the following day, but Sarah told me that there was a couple already sleeping in the spare bedroom. This was no big deal, however, as I had crashed on her couch more than a few times in the past.

But as I made myself comfortable on the sofa for some sleep, Sarah suddenly became agitated and quite animated. She crawled around on the floor like a mad woman, babbling about how "some day" she was going to get away from everything and everyone and have it made. I attempted to ignore her, hoping she would eventually wind down from her drunken state and go to sleep, but soon she was crawling right up to me on the couch and ranting even more.

"Someday I'm going to be rich," she panted. "My daughter Tiffany is going to be rich and famous and I'll have it made." I told her that she should go to sleep, that she would feel better in the morning. Then she said the words that have stuck with me ever since that night: "You know how I know all this? It's because I talk to the Devil. He said he's going to make Tiffany famous and that we're both going to be rich."

Now Sarah isn't a bad person—and I certainly doubted that she seriously worshipped Satan—but she wasn't the brightest of individuals. Why she was saying such bizarre things was beyond me. But say these things she did—and for quite a while before finally winding down and deciding to go to bed. At that point, she slowly got up off the floor and made her way to the adjoining bedroom. She then asked, "Do you mind bringing the baby into the bedroom for me?"

I said that I didn't, so I picked up the entire bassinet and carried it into the bedroom. I placed it a few feet from the bed (little Tiffany was sound asleep) and left as Sarah was crawling under the covers. I then went to the couch, made myself comfortable, and fell fast asleep. The next thing I knew it was morning and there was a knock on the front door, quickly followed by screams of utter terror.

I sat up quickly on the couch trying to comprehend what was happening. The couple that was sleeping in the guest bedroom shot by me in a mad dash into the bedroom to check on Sarah. This prompted a second set of screams.

Meanwhile, the knocking on the door became frantic. So I got up and opened the front door in a hurry; it was my friend ready to take us to our job interviews. I then shot into Sarah's room to see why they were all screaming. Of course, I now wish that I hadn't.

Poor baby Tiffany was lying in her bassinet and she was blue. She had died during the night. And if this wasn't bad enough, it was the state of the child that has stuck with me for all these years. The baby was lying on her back with her back arched and her arms up in the air—almost as if she was warding off someone or reaching for something. Her little head was back and her mouth was still open as if she had been screaming or gasping for air.

As everyone tried to calm Sarah down and comfort her, I said that I would go call an ambulance. Naturally, Sarah had no phone in the trailer so I would have to go to Tara's house to call the ambulance. Since I did not want to be the one to tell Tara (or her mother) that little Tiffany was dead, I told them that the baby was unresponsive and needed an ambulance. But it was completely clear from looking at the body that the baby had been dead for a while.

My friend and I then left for our interviews as the ambulance was en route to the trailer. Once we were finished, I returned to Tara's house to find the family grieving over their loss. Sarah was a complete wreck.

We were soon informed by the police that the baby's father was going to be released from the county prison for forty-eight hours to attend the funeral and grieve, and it wasn't long before he was at the home and they were all planning the funeral for the baby. Still shook up by the whole affair, I thought it best to let the family have some alone time, so I left and went home.

The following day, I returned again to visit with Tara and found the baby's father in tears on the front porch. I asked him if he was all right, and he responded with a terrifying story. He stated that he had gone to the trailer to pick up some clothes for the baby to be buried in, along with some appropriate clothes for Sarah to wear to the funeral.

While he was gathering the items, he suddenly heard a disturbing sound: the loud cries of an infant. And they were coming from the bedroom where he was standing. He immediately dropped the clothes and fled the scene. He then asked if I would mind going over to pick up the items for him; they would be waiting where he left them in the bedroom floor of the trailer ...

Reluctantly, I agreed. So I again called upon my buddy to go with me to the trailer (there was no way I was going in there alone). When we arrived, the door to the trailer was wide open. In his haste to escape, the father had not shut the door.

Cautiously, the two of us went inside and made our way to the bedroom. The clothes were right on the floor where they were supposed to be. And though we did not hear a baby crying in the trailer, we still gathered the items as quickly as we could and fled the premises as if we had.

In the weeks that followed, the horror and sorrow of the tragic death began to fade and life went on for everyone. The father went back to jail, the baby was buried, and we all tried to get past the horrific experience. As for Sarah, she could no longer stand to live in the trailer, so she moved back in with the family. It was at about this point that I started experiencing a horrible, yet persistent, recurring nightmare.

In this dream, I was reliving the events of the night that Tiffany had died: I walked Tara home, I returned to the trailer to find Sarah ranting about the Devil, and then

I went to sleep on the couch. But this is where the dream threw a curveball.

Instead of sleeping soundly on the couch till the following morning, I heard the sounds of the baby crying hysterically filling the air. In my dream, I'm lying on the couch and thinking, "Why doesn't Sarah pick up the baby? Doesn't she hear her crying in there?" Then, after what seems like an eternity, the crying suddenly halts. The dream ends with the knock on the front door and Sarah's scream.

I probably don't have to tell you that this dream messed with my head. Could I have slept right through a baby crying hysterically in the adjoining room? I doubted it, but it could have been possible. I then began to feel guilty. If I had woken up, I could have picked up the baby—or at least told Sarah to do so. If, of course, this had happened at all. There was just no way to know for sure. Either way, the dream haunted me to no end.

After enduring this recurring nightmare for a week, I decided to talk to Sarah about it, even though I thought it would be a difficult conversation. The coroner had already said the baby died of "crib death," but even hinting that the baby's death could have been prevented might open up a whole new can of bad worms.

When I approached Sarah and broached the subject of that night, I was surprised to find her almost cheerful. I asked her why she was in a good mood and was staggered yet again by a completely unexpected answer. She told me that the Devil had taken her baby away to teach her a lesson about invoking his name. He had taken Tiffany away and, according to her, now given her back to her. What?!

Apparently, the very day that Tiffany had died, Sarah had had sex with the briefly freed father of the baby. From this one union she said she was now pregnant. And according to the girl, she was pregnant once again with Tiffany, returned to her by the Devil. I, of course, was convinced Sarah had snapped and that she was in serious need of psychological counseling. And I told this very thing to Tara and her family. But guess what?

Sarah would go on to have another baby girl, she would name the new baby Tiffany, and she would tell everyone that this was her first baby reincarnated! Keep in mind that Tiffany II was conceived on the very day that Tiffany I had passed away in the early morning hours!

Even back then, in my youth, I was a logical person. I did not truly believe that the Devil had anything to do with the death of one baby or the birth of another. But I'd be lying if I said that there wasn't a nagging, small percentage of my brain that wasn't frightened by the thought of just such a thing having happened.

Now, as I was working on a case that would, potentially, have me facing something demonic again in the near future, all my old fears and experiences were rushing back to me. It would be all I could do to keep focused on the factual, logical elements of the investigation and to not obsess over the strange things that were happening at the Martin property, as well as at my own home.

7

THE SECOND VISIT

The drive back into the Deep South wasn't any easier the second time around—even with me bringing back some interesting audio clips and a photo for Joanne to review. But after drinking a Waffle House worth of coffee, I eventually found myself pulling into the local Unitarian church's parking lot for my meeting with our house-blesser, Frank, the Unitarian minister from Alabama.

After discussing the particulars of the Martin case with Frank via email, he had thought it best if we met outside the Martin household prior to his arrival. This would give him the chance to check out the evidence I had gathered, as well as to hear some firsthand tales from Terri and her crew. Frank would also have the opportunity to run down what he had in mind for his visit to the trailer.

The minister met me at the door of the church with a smile and, once we were past the hellos and pleasantries, I briefed him on what, exactly, he would be getting into at the Martin house. He never blinked an eye as I detailed the environment and situation at the residence.

I watched him closely as I described the questionable living conditions, the myriad paranormal experiences, and gave a rather vivid depiction of the residents. His expression never changed. When I pointed out that he seemed rather calm about all the information that I was feeding him, he simply said, "I preach in Alabama. I've seen it all."

It was only a few moments later when the members of the Mississippi team arrived at the church, so soon we all sat down to look at the evidence I had gathered during my first evening at the trailer.

It was kind of fun to watch the expressions on the minister's face change as I played the EVPs I had captured with my audio recorders. It was a mixture of surprise, intrigue, and disbelief. Pretty much what I experienced when I first heard the odd voices. When I got to the mysterious photo, however, Terri and Patricia informed me that they believed they had debunked the image.

After I had sent it to them via email, they were so excited about the photo that they had immediately revisited the trailer. They found that when they looked at an air-conditioning unit from the angle I had taken the picture, it eerily resembled the "eyes" in the photograph. As a result, they came to the conclusion the photo didn't contain anything of a paranormal nature.

Inwardly, I was quietly relieved that there was an explanation for the photo—mostly because I didn't want to see the effect it would have on Joanne and company. She was panicked enough without having a photograph to refer to! But I would have a look at the air conditioner for myself once I got back to the trailer.

Photo aside, though, we all decided that it would probably be best for the minister to meet Joanne and her family before we investigated the trailer that evening, and then he could return to perform the house blessing the following day once he was finished with his Sunday sermon (in addition to preaching in Alabama, he worked occasionally at a local Unitarian church as well—hence the reason he was available to perform the blessing in Mississippi).

So after we were through with the obligatory briefings at the church, Terri gave Frank the same warnings about the Martin trailer that she had passed on to me prior to my first visit. Then we packed up all the gear and convoyed over to the Martin residence.

The Scene of the Crime

We arrived at the trailer to find Joanne waving at us from the driveway like we were relatives visiting for the weekend. As we parked in front of the residence, I noticed that the grass and surrounding foliage were in a terrible state and that the trailer was missing another window (I would later learn that this broken window was the result of vandalism). With a deep breath I exited the vehicle, greeted Joanne, and suggested that we all go inside to talk. This was an immediate mistake.

If it was possible, the home was in even worse condition than it was on my first visit. Apparently, shortly after my first investigation, Tim and Sarah had moved out of the trailer.

According to them, they were simply tired of dealing with the all the scary activity. And since Joanne and her two young daughters were now left alone, they too suddenly found the environment to be too frightening to live in. As a result, they had also moved out to stay with some nearby relatives.

But the worst news was yet to come: Since nobody had been living in the home for some time, Joanne had turned off the power, so we would be working entirely from battery power. This was a detail that would have been nice to have before driving down, as I could have prepared for the situation by bringing more batteries. Now I would have to be more strategic about where I placed my gear and how long I let the audio and video gear run in one location.

Furthermore, with no air conditioning or fans, the place was sweltering. Spending even a few minutes inside the massive heat-box produced rivers of sweat and induced gasps for air. There would be no way we could seriously perform an investigation during the daylight hours.

We would have to wait until sundown before working inside.

I asked Joanne how often she had visited the place since she had moved out, and was told "never." Only a cousin had been by to check—and he had done that only once. According to her, this male relative had scoffed at her claims regarding the property, so he planned to spend the night alone in the trailer. Much to her amusement, he didn't even make it until nightfall.

He reported that he had entered the residence, dropped his overnight bag, and then proceeded to look around the trailer for ghosts when he heard a loud thud. He rushed back into the living room to find that his bag had been thrown across the room. This was more than enough proof for him, so he grabbed his things and fled. He had no intention of waiting around to actually see a ghost!

As Patricia introduced Frank to Joanne, I decided to take a look at the area in front of the trailer that contained the "face" in my mysterious photo. It didn't take long to see how the air conditioner could be the phantom eyes in the photograph (there were two square areas on the side of the unit that match up with where the eyes were in the photo)—but I couldn't figure out what anything else in the photo could be.

There was clearly a tree branch in front of the figure in the photo, but any kind of material that would make the hair and beard on the figure's head was nowhere to be found. The tree branch (as well as the whole tree) that was in the photo was bereft of any leaves or branches that could be mistaken for a spirit. If the eyes were the air conditioner, then what was making up the rest of the figure's features? Suddenly I was not so sure the photo was completely debunked.

I was unsure enough of the authenticity, though, that it justified me not showing it to Joanne (I really didn't want to give her another reason to be afraid), but I would have to get some more opinions on the photograph before making a final decision. After I snapped a few new reference photos, I went back inside the trailer scratching my head.

Now that everyone had met each other, I decided to formally interview Joanne again for the minister's benefit. I also wanted to interview young Julie this time, so while Terri left to go pick her up, I switched on an audio recorder and began going over the details with Joanne again regarding the haunting of the house.

Now that I had thought about the case extensively while reviewing my footage I captured the first time around (as well as during two lengthy drives into Mississippi), I was armed with a whole new batch of fresh questions and ready to learn more about the background of this case.

More Details

Before Joanne could get too comfortable with talking to all of us, I decided I would immediately attempt to get more information about the entity "John." Was there any reason to believe that there was such a spirit in the house other than "Tim said so"?

After a moment of deep thought, Joanne revealed more details about the family rumors that had circulated down through the years regarding the possible murder of a local black man named John. In fact, there were three such rumors. They went like this:

1. One night Joanne's grandfather was preparing for bed when he heard a commotion coming from the slaughterhouse/shed. Grabbing a gun, he went out to check on the noise and caught a black man in the act of stealing meat from the smoker. He promptly shot the intruder, who died on the spot. This could have possibly been John.

2. A relative once told Joanne a tale involving a vagrant who wandered onto the family property from a set of nearby train tracks. Much like the first version of the family rumor, the man was killed while trespassing. Again, this could be John.

3. It's possible that John was a neighbor who supposedly lived down the way. Back in the 1940s or so, telephones in the area were scarce, so John came knocking on the door of Joanne's grandfather, who lived on the property at the time, wanting to use his phone. According to this version of the story, John was promptly beaten to a pulp, taken to the shed/

slaughterhouse (the place that's still barely standing in front of the trailer), and murdered. It is this version of the story that Tim claimed to have gotten during one of his possessions—adding details such as John being bound with barbed wire, his throat being cut, and his body being buried in the area behind where the original house once stood.

Though Joanne wasn't sure which, if any, of the stories were true, she certainly believed (thanks to Tim) that there was a John present in the home. This new information was disturbing to me on a few levels. If there was, indeed, a murder, this would have to be reported to the local authorities—even if it happened more than half a century ago. With such a sparse local population, if a man had gone missing, there was a good chance he would still have family in the area. And I was quite sure that they'd like to know what happened to him!

I asked Joanne if she even thought her grandfather was capable of such a thing. To this, she would only say that there was a history of abuse that ran through her family and that such a crime could most definitely have occurred with him or any number of her relatives that lived in the area. (Adding on to this information is the fact that the trailer's land has been in her family for over 150 years, so there had been plenty of generations of Martins living there to do such a thing.)

After hearing all this, I decided to let Frank have a moment alone with Joanne to counsel her. Speaking about her
relatives seemed to upset her. While he did this, I pulled
the Mississippi crew aside and mentioned that we might
have to let the local police know about these rumors; Tom
and Blake were friends with several officers in the sheriff's
department, so they would definitely bring it up with them
to see if it warranted further legal attention. This made me
feel better about the situation, though I still hated the idea
that there could be a family in the vicinity who was missing
a loved one.

When I returned to the conversation between Frank
and Joanne, they were talking about the activity she had
witnessed in the trailer. I listened as she told Frank the same
basic stories that we had briefed him on earlier that day.
But before she could finish with her narrative, I thought
this might be a good time to address another issue I had
with the first investigation: the occult/magical paraphernalia scattered about the home. So I quickly interrupted their
conversation and asked her straight out, "Tell me about the
magic herbs and wand we found while we were here."

With a sheepish grin, Joanne freely admitted that she
had "dabbled" a bit in various sorts of religion—but, again,
reiterated that she believed in almost everything. According to her, most of this dabbling occurred after the trailer
was already haunted, and this was just one of the ways they
had tried to cope with it. And from the way she was telling

me all of this ("we tried," "we were scared," etc.), it was clear that she had included her daughters in these acts.

I was still digesting all this information when the front door slammed shut with a bang, startling everyone in the kitchen. A quick "Sorry!" came from the living room. Terri had returned with Julie for my interview. Frank gave a nervous laugh as the young girl was brought forth for introductions.

As Frank met with Julie for the first time, I decided to go over my audio findings from the first visit to the trailer with Joanne. I went over each audio clip with her, explaining what an EVP was and what to listen for. She nodded and smiled as each piece of evidence was presented—and I could tell by the expression on her face that she was grateful to have something tangible to back up her claims.

Though I feared that my evidence might make her even more uneasy in the home, all I saw on her face was relief. Finally, someone understood and believed her. I did not show her the photo, however—again, I was not sure the photo was something paranormal or if I was simply matrixing something out of nothing. So no mention was made. Once we were finished with the audio clips, though, I went into the living room to meet with Julie for myself.

Interviewing Julie

Speaking to Julie was like speaking to a fully grown woman in miniature form. Patricia, one of the Mississippi investigators, had described the girl as having an "old soul"—and now I had to agree. Of course, when you grow up in a dysfunctional household, you pretty much have to grow up fast and, at the very least, learn how to take care of yourself. And it was clear that she had done this.

Once we had all gotten comfortable in the kitchen (or at least as comfortable as you can be when it's over 90 degrees with high humidity), I thought I'd start the conversation with her by focusing on the most pertinent subject to my investigation: Emily.

I had thought that speaking about Emily might be a difficult thing for Julie so I wanted to get it over with as quickly as possible. It turned out that the exact opposite was true; Julie liked talking about Emily. You might even say she loved it.

Julie described speaking to the dead girl as if it was an ongoing conversation that she had been having with the spirit since she was about four years old. When I asked for details concerning Emily, I was told that she had "blonde hair" and that she "wore a dress"—the same description that Joanne had given me during my first visit.

I asked why the spirit of the girl was in their home. According to Julie, Emily had drowned in a nearby creek and now her spirit was wandering the area, looking for her family, which was now long gone. I asked Julie how she knew Emily's family was long gone. "Well," she pointed out, "Emily wears an old-time dress." Ahh…

As I spoke with the young girl, another thing became crystal clear: Julie was a fan of paranormal television. She threw around terms like "intelligent spirit," "residual haunting," and "paranormal activity" like a seasoned ghost hunter.

And, along with her mother, Julie had delved into the basics of magic. In fact, the wand we had come across during the first investigation was actually made by Julie for her own personal use. I made a note of this and found myself now beginning to wonder how much of what was happening around them (or at least their opinion of what was happening) was being influenced by what they had been watching on television.

All too often, when people experience strange things, they turn to paranormal programs and books for answers. But since most people lack any real experience dealing with such matters, they often come to erroneous conclusions or they blow certain events out of proportion. As a result, common-sense answers are often overlooked—especially if there's a more exciting answer that's similar to what they saw last week on TV!

After I wrapped up the interview with Julie, Terri and Patricia pulled me aside and told me something else about the young girl: Julie was known by local children her own age to be quite promiscuous. Terri's son went to school with Julie and knew a lot about the girl—and Terri and Tom had actually caught the nude Julie attempting to seduce their son in their own house!

While I found this information to be disturbing on a whole new level, it did seem to confirm that there was a young girl within the throes of puberty in the trailer—a classic ingredient for poltergeist activity. It also confirmed, though, that Julie craved attention and that she might be trying to get it any way that she could.

Having finished with my interview, I called Joanne into the room with us. With Julie and Joanne both being present together with me for the first time, I decided it would be a good time to broach the subject of Keith again.

I wanted to know if either of them had actually seen anything that would indicate that Julie's dead father was in the trailer. Again, at this point, this particular haunting was based entirely on Tim's word. So I asked them, "Other than Tim telling you that Keith is here in the trailer, what makes you think he is here?"

To my amazement, Joanne became indignant and answered me by pointing at Julie and saying, "Grab her titty and see what happens!"

What do you say to an answer like that? The implication was that if I acted in such a manner to Julie, the spirit of Keith would retaliate in some way. Of course there would be no underage titty-grabbing happening any time soon, so I thought this might be a good time to end the interviews. With more than a few laughs erupting around me, I went outside for a breath of fresh air.

At this point, I was pretty much through with interviewing everyone, so I decided it was probably a good time for us all to go grab some food. We would need to fuel up for another evening of investigating and the trailer still needed to cool down considerably.

But before we left, I decided to go ahead and set up a couple audio recorders in the trailer to run during our absence. It was a great opportunity to catch some EVPs without anyone being on the premises. Once this was done, we all loaded up in the vehicles again to go into town for some food at a local pizzeria.

Dinner and the Ride Home

Our meal went pretty much like any other and ended with us saying goodbye to Frank for the night. He promised to contact us after his Sunday services the following day before returning to the house to perform the blessing.

But as he sped off into the night, things took another interesting turn; Joanne asked if she and Julie could ride with me back to the trailer (they had commuted to the restaurant with Terri and Tom). I stammered an "okay," and soon we were off.

We were in the car for maybe two minutes when Joanne began asking me how I "went about" shooting a movie. She had heard from Terri and Patricia that I was involved with *Ghosts of War* (a documentary I produced/directed about haunted Civil War sites) and she was interested in making a movie about her ordeal in the trailer. I don't have to say that, at this point, alarm bells were going off all over the place. She was actually asking how they could capitalize on their haunting!

Giving her the benefit of the doubt (instant television/movie fame is one of the bad side effects of paranormal reality TV), I told her that making a feature film is quite difficult and that it can cost a lot of money. I understood that Joanne and her family were in dire financial straits; she was a single parent raising her kids with a difficult budget, a home that was fast becoming unlivable, and (of all things) a haunting to contend with. Of course she would want to explore the possibility of improving their lives financially.

This led us into a whole conversation that involved me explaining the production process of movies and the need for her to write out her story so that a script could be formed (it seemed she was speaking of a narrative feature rather than a documentary). She then told me that one of her daughters was an actor in Austin, Texas, and that she'd like for her to have work.

Again, I gave Joanne the benefit of the doubt and just assumed that her questions about a movie was just her desire to help out her daughter in Austin with some work. I did not want to think that she, or anyone else in the home, was attempting to use their ordeal to simply make a profit. Either way, I pushed all this out of my mind as I pulled up in the driveway of the trailer.

I'd just have to get back to the basics; I knew from my first investigation and review that the place *was* most likely haunted. In the end, it would be the evidence gathered from my investigations that would determine any validity to any/all claims being made—not any hasty judgments made by me or anyone else concerning the intentions of the household.

With the last remnants of daylight hovering on the horizon, we quickly unloaded the remainder of our equipment for the night while Joanne and Julie made their way to a relative's house that was just a short distance away. The ghost hunt was on!

The Second Investigation

Much like the first investigation, we spent the first part of the evening setting up additional audio recorders and video gear while staking out various areas of the trailer for activity (often called a "vigil" in the paranormal world). Blake and I manned the master bedroom, while the remaining team members went to do some EVP work in the bedrooms at the back of the trailer.

After we settled in, we almost immediately began to hear a strange scratching sound coming from the kitchen. Armed with a couple of EMF detectors, we cautiously approached the area. The sound was coming from the kitchen sink. The sudden elation that something paranormal might be happening quickly went south, though, when we discovered it was a mouse trapped in an empty two-liter soda bottle. Rats!

We returned to the master bedroom and concentrated on trying to get another rumble—or at least some EVPs—on audio. After about an hour with nothing discernible happening around us, we rallied up with the other team members so that we could rotate to different areas of the trailer.

Breaking off on my own, I soon found myself in the rear room of the trailer—an area that seemed to function as a second living room, though was now a general dumping area for miscellaneous objects. This was also the place where we had spotted the various occult/magic objects during our first visit. While I performed some EVP work there, I decided to take a closer look at the various items scattered about the room.

Besides the same assorted bottles of herbs and oils that we saw the first time we investigated, I found an odd bottle of powdered incense. Upon examination, the scent of the incense was actually called "Exorcism." If Joanne and her family were not instigating any of the activity in this house—nor had any belief it was anything inhuman—why were they purchasing this kind of incense? Suddenly I was angry.

Clearly Joanne was saying one thing and doing another. Not only did I now believe she was creating—or at least exacerbating—all the activity in the trailer herself, but I was sure she was manipulating us and the information she divulged to get herself more attention than a simple haunting warranted. I crammed the bottle of incense in my pocket, determined to confront Joanne about it later that evening.

About an hour after I discovered the incense, Terri and Patricia gave a shout from the trailer's bathroom. They, too, had found an interesting item: a makeshift Ouija board drawn onto the bathroom floor. It was drawn on the wooden floor under some loose carpet, but was plainly visible to everyone present (even though it looked to have been made using a ballpoint pen or small marker).

This was just too much now. It's one thing to believe you are assisting a victim with a haunting—it's quite another to find out that, not only are they performing acts that could possibly *cause* or invite a haunting, but they are hiding this information from the investigators.

But I was also struck again by the similarities of this case to the Cottage City, Maryland, exorcism. The activity that plagued the poor young man (and that led to an exorcism) began in part because of the use of a Ouija board and séances. The Ouija board part was even included in the movie, *The Exorcist.* All that was missing in this case was the séance!

Once again, I had a good reason to confront Joanne. Were the details just coincidentally similar to the exorcism case or was this yet another detail that they may have picked up from watching the movie and decided to try it in their home? Either way, it was one more example of how the Martins were not being completely truthful with us. Luckily, the whole evening wouldn't be discoveries of the bad sort.

Not long after uncovering the Ouija, we started getting activity in the long hallway outside the bedroom doors. This was the same area that I had witnessed the shadow figure in during my first time around. Much like the first trip to the house, we found a strange reading on a K2 EMF detector—only this time it was sustained. This was especially interesting because there was no power at all in the trailer to cause a false or natural reading.

Over the course of about an hour, we managed to follow a fairly contained energy source at it roamed be-

tween several rooms of the trailer. The K2 would spike in
the kitchen, I'd ask a few EVP questions, and then the meter
would go flat—as if it had fled the room. Then a quick search
of the area would find the energy in a new spot.

This impromptu game of hide-and-seek went on for
quite a while, but, eventually, the energy dissipated entirely
and we couldn't find it any more. I was just hoping we got
something on our audio recorders during this extended
Q&A/chase period.

After this burst of activity, not much else seemed to be
happening. We set up motion detectors, we peered through
camcorders, and we patrolled the place almost constantly
with EMF detectors and digital thermometers. Nothing.

With the night winding down, we decided we may
as well start packing up the gear. The Mississippi team
seemed a little disappointed that the evening had been
relatively slow, but I know from past experience that in
a lot of cases things just *seem* to be slow, but lots of great
evidence gets captured on the audio and video devices. I
hoped that this would be the case again.

Once we were finished packing up for the evening,
Joanne returned to the trailer to lock up. I immediately
sat her down and confronted her about the incense and
Ouija board.

At first she used the "defense" argument; she claimed
she had purchased the incense to ward off any possible
spirits and that she didn't know who had drawn the Ouija
on the bathroom floor (the drawing had been covered by

a rug/piece of linoleum, but was now clearly visible—even to Joanne).

After I pressed her for a bit, she finally did admit that the family might be to blame for some of the things going on, though she still believed John had been around since her grandfather's days on the property. She also confessed that not long after they had all moved into the trailer, one of her older daughters (the actor in Austin) had decided to host an impromptu séance in the trailer with a couple of her friends.

According to Joanne, they were getting nowhere with the séance until they decided to try to speak to the spirit of Marilyn Monroe. It was then that things began to happen—things like a picture flying off the wall in front of the now-terrified girls. The séance was quickly ended at that point, and (interestingly) it wouldn't be long before young Julie would start seeing and hearing Emily.

I was dumbstruck. I had joked earlier that evening with the Mississippi team that a séance was the last missing piece to this case having "everything possible" that could cause their haunting to take place. It was also another key element to the exorcist case as I mentioned before. The similarities now were getting ridiculous; either they were on the same path as the Cottage City, Maryland, family or Joanne's family had somehow read about the previous case and was actually attempting to duplicate the happenings.

I, of course, found this hard to believe. While some folks may be a little to blame for getting into ghosts too much, I have yet to meet anyone who would willingly wish demonic infestation upon themselves! And on another note, the book that detailed the particulars of the séance was *Possessed*, not *The Exorcist*. Would Joanne even know there was a second book about the story? I doubted it.

So the family had done a séance in the trailer. Was Marilyn Monroe now haunting the trailer along with the rest of the ghosts there? Yeah, right… Could the specter of Emily have "come through" while they were attempting to speak to Marilyn? Possibly. With my brain now reeling with the various elements affecting this case, I decided to wrap up for the night. I would need several days back in the comfort of my own home to decipher all the information I had ingested over the evening—not to mention to go over all the data I had collected.

Blessing the Home

Though I would already be on the road back to Memphis when the minister visited the trailer for the blessing the following day, I would hear all about the experience from Terri via telephone. Once Frank had finished his duties at the local church on Sunday, he joined the Mississippi group at the trailer and, once again, talked with Joanne about the blessing.

When he had finished explaining how he would go about the task, he began making his way room to room throughout the trailer, stopping to bless each individual area. According to Terri and Patricia, everything was going pretty much as expected until Frank saw something strange for himself.

He had just stepped into the hallway that leads back to the second family room (the "magic room") when he saw a large, black shape—possibly a figure—move into that area. He didn't want to alarm Joanne, so he said nothing, but when he got to that particular room and performed the blessing there, he actually witnessed the large, black mass move up from the floor and pass through the ceiling!

This was startling, but he continued blessing the home and managed to finish up without another incident occurring. So, after a few quick goodbyes, he was on his way with a nice, scary story to tell of his own experience in the Martin residence.

I asked Terri if Frank had placed any significance to the black mass moving, seemingly, out of the trailer. She said that Frank had not indicated any special significance. I thanked her and hung up my phone. I would have to email Frank again once I was home to get his thoughts about the affair.

Did the exiting mass mean at least one of the spirits left? Or was the entity simply avoiding the clergyman who was reading scripture in the room? Who knows? Ironically, it wasn't long after the blessing that Joanne told the Mississippi team that the place was still haunted; she said that she was on her way down the driveway to pick up her mail the day following the blessing when she heard the sounds of gravel falling around her and all-too-familiar footsteps following her ...

8

GETTING CLARITY

I returned home even more confused than usual. Tired and confused. The two investigations at the Martin home had turned up a mixed batch of conflicting information and nothing seemed to strictly adhere to any one type of paranormal activity. With my head spinning from all of the possibilities, I decided it might be best to make a pro/con list concerning the question, "Is the Martin trailer haunted?"

Grabbing a pen and paper, I sat down and began to tally up the facts that supported the idea that something of a paranormal nature was happening on the property. Here are the pro-haunting things I came up with:

1. Multiple witnesses had seen and heard things in the trailer that are typically associated with a haunting. And while I could discount some of the

testimony (especially the possibly drug-induced eyewitness accounts), activity was also witnessed by seasoned paranormal investigators—including myself! These things included objects moving (such as the utensil flying through the air), disembodied voices, and sightings of an apparition (the ghost girl in the window and several instances of a shadowy figure/shape).

2. Evidence gathered at the trailer seemed to support the idea that something paranormal is happening. Though I couldn't reliably call the photograph taken of the "face" paranormal, I had captured at least two voices—one male, one female—on audio during my first investigation. And the audio of the loud rumble can be debated by no one!

3. The Martin family history, as well as local history, supports the idea that something traumatic (possibly murder) may have happened on the property. With the area being a hotbed for racially driven crime in the past—and local law enforcement confirming that the neighboring forest was once a popular spot for such activity—it is definitely within the realm of possibility that a "John" could have been murdered there. And Joanne herself admitted that members of her family were entirely capable of committing such an atrocity.

4. Joanne confirmed that in the past there had been a séance, the use of a Ouija board, and occult/magic rituals all performed in the trailer. As documented during my visit, there were still items related to these activities on the premises. This included the Ouija board drawn on the bathroom floor, herbs used for magical purposes, the presence of incense (one expressly used for exorcism), a ward/mandala hanging on a wall, and a magic wand carved with some sort of runes.

5. Several types of rare activity most likely occurred at the site. These acts included the phantom rock-throwing that was witnessed by deputies, materialization of objects such as coins (which happened at least twice) and the watch that appeared in the master bedroom, and the spontaneous combustion that sent the television set into flames and then through one of the front windows—though that act was not paranormal.

These seemed to be the five strongest arguments for a haunting taking place in the Martin property. Before moving on to the cons, though, I decided to make a "maybe" list. This list would itemize the events and occurrences that were alleged, but not much in the way of evidence seemed to support them. Here are the maybes:

1. A young girl named Emily could be haunting the house. Though a female face had been witnessed peering in one window—and I had EVPs of a female voice—there was nothing that definitively pointed to an entity being a child named Emily. Furthermore, there was no supporting evidence of any Emily drowning in the area. All the information regarding an Emily came from Julie and Julie alone.

2. Julie's father Keith could be haunting the house. Anything to do with Keith came from "feelings" that the residents there had; they *felt* like Keith was there protecting his daughter. And all information/ details provided about Keith being in the trailer came from an entirely unreliable witness: Tim. I had captured a few EVPs of a male voice—but there was no way to know if the voice was Keith, John, or simply some other male entity (there's no telling how many Martin family members had perished on the family land over the decades).

3. Several types of activity had happened only once or twice and/or were unable to be documented or recorded. These events included the strange scents of rotten eggs and feces that had appeared during the worst of the activity, but also included all the instances I detailed where something happened with only a single person in the home to see it.

Now came the cons—the things that hurt the case for the Martin family experiencing a haunting. They are few, but they are big ones…

1. Joanne Martin. She is her own worst enemy. She had conveniently left out key pieces of information throughout the investigation, she had seemingly drawn upon events from horror movies to build support for her home being haunted (such an instance would be the demonic moth incident), and worst of all, she clearly had at least contributed to her own situation by allowing her family to indulge in séances, the use of a makeshift Ouija board and incenses, and the like. But worse than all this, she wanted to capitalize on what was, according to her, terrifying her family. This was confirmed by her interest in wanting to shoot a movie about her family's ordeal—even if it was for a good reason (improving her family's financial situation, etc.).

2. The use of drugs. With paraphernalia littering the home, it was obvious that some members of the household were quite probably under the influence of drugs when some (or all) of the activity was happening in the trailer. How reliable could such people be as witnesses? I hoped that Julie and Katie were free of such influences, but nobody else in the household could be ruled out in this regard.

3. Conflicting information and rarity of activity.
   While this cannot definitively be called a "con," it
   still has to be noted as a negative aspect of this case.
   Interviews with the members of the household
   had brought to light aspects of poltergeist activity,
   possessions, and (possibly) demonic activity, and
   even suggested that multiple types of sometimes
   extremely rare activity were occurring in the home
   (as mentioned above). How could one double-wide
   trailer in the heart of the Mississippi delta have so
   much going on? Was it possible?

Just writing down all this information and detailing
what I had gathered from my two trips was cathartic.
Though I still had no explanation for what was happening
at the Martin property, it was nice having all the facts and
details listed in front of me. I felt like I could now move forward and take a look at the audio, photographic, and video
data that I had collected during my second visit.

Since I had been limited to the battery power I had
on hand during the second investigation, there was significantly less to go over this time around. This would get
no complaints from me, however…

Back to the Drawing Board

With one successful session of reviewing evidence under
my belt, the second go at it was tackled with a bit more
enthusiasm, though peppered with the occasional yawn.

It helped to know going in that I had already captured some great evidence at this location, so this increased my odds of getting something great this time around, too.

As I have learned in the past, even though you may have had a dead investigation (excuse the pun), careful attention must still be given to the data collected during any investigation. As with the Devil's Backbone case mentioned earlier in the book, you never know what you will end up with.

In addition to all this, I was also motivated by the fact that, since I had been on a battery-powered excursion, it meant that I could wrap up my review in a mere three days instead of five or six. Sweet! So, once again, I sat down at the computer, sipped coffee, listened to hours of audio, watched hours of video, and sifted through hundreds of still photographs. All with the hope of finding a definitive piece of evidence that would point me in the right direction with this case.

As I slowly waded my way through all the files on my computer, it became clear that this review was going to be basically like every other one I had done in the past: photographs would mostly serve as reference material, video would be boring and eventless, and audio would be the bread-and-butter of the trip. Big surprise.

The second batch of files yielded no video evidence—and unlike the photo of the "face" captured during my first visit, there would be no interesting images to dissect this time around. As is the case with so many investigations, the evidence would have to come from the hours of audio recordings captured at the site.

More Findings

The first interesting audio clip I found during the review was captured while performing an EVP session in the master bedroom. Patricia and Terri were attempting to communicate with the entity called John when they thought they heard a voice in the room with them. Unfortunately, other investigators were chattering away in the next room, so they had a hard time hearing what was happening. Fortunately the audio recorder in the room had no such difficulty.

On the recorded audio, you can clearly hear Patricia state that she cannot hear over the people in the next room, so Terri gets up and goes to the door to shush them. Right after Terri admonishes the neighboring investigators, you can clearly hear a harsh, whispered voice say, "Shut up!" Apparently one of the entities in the trailer was as frustrated with the chatty investigators as Patricia and Terri were!

I made a note to contact Patricia with this particular EVP just to make sure it wasn't her or Terri chiding the talkers (even though the voice doesn't sound female) and moved on to more of the audio. It wasn't long before I heard the next interesting EVP.

This one was captured in Julie's bedroom—when it was completely empty. It was faint, but definitely there: a long breath and the sound of a girl humming. The voice sounded young, like a small girl, but Julie was not there during the recording. A minute or so later, on the same recorder, the voice is followed by the clear sound of something hard banging/moving in the bedroom.

Around the same time these particular clips were captured, a second audio recorder—this time in the second family room—turned up a male voice while Patricia, Terri, and I were doing some EVP work.

You can clearly hear a gasping voice say two quick words, though I have not been able to decipher what's being said (another typical occurrence in the paranormal field). I had to suppress the urge to try and form words out of the syllables. Though I knew that whatever I *thought* was being said, it could be debated by others and would most likely be a form of audio matrixing (or wishful thinking).

This same EVP session would also reveal a second piece of evidence. Patricia was attempting to speak to the spirit of Emily. She was asking why Emily was there in the trailer and if she could "see the light." This question was answered by a young female voice quickly saying either "Uh huh, uh huh" or "Unh uh, unh uh." My instinct says it's the latter because the voice sounds distressed rather than upbeat (which I would hope would be the attitude associated with "seeing the light").

The part of the audio review that paid off the most for me, though, was the portion that was captured during our little K2 chase between Julie's bedroom and the bathroom. While we were pursuing the strange burst of energy that seemed to be avoiding us, the audio captured a loud and clear EVP of a young girl. It is clearly a frustrated sigh that attests to the fact that this particular entity was attempting to get away from us. And though the spirit did, indeed, get away, we had managed to get evidence on our audio recorder.

A few hours later into my review of the audio, I found even more. Besides the EVPs already noted, two more interesting clips were captured on the audio recorder that was placed in the trailer's kitchen. During what was clearly the chase of the entity with the EMF detector (an act that all the investigators present were participating in), the sounds of whispered voices were recorded in the kitchen.

At first, the words are unintelligible. Then there's the clear phrase, "I know it." It was almost as if there was an otherworldly discussion going on in the kitchen while we were working just down the hall—a rather spooky-sounding discussion.

Later on, on the same audio recorder, the sounds of Joanne returning to the trailer can be heard. I had left it running as we wrapped up the investigation for the night. This is a practice I recommend for investigators in general; many times over the years I have gotten my best EVPs/evidence during our set-up or tear-down of the gear. I attribute this, once again, to the fact that we are "ignoring" the spirits during these periods.

Once we were packed up, I had sat down with the other investigators and Joanne to confront her about the make-shift Ouija board and exorcism incense. You can hear all of this in the recording. At one point, Joanne began to reiterate some of the facts regarding the land's history and was mentioning her grandfather when a strange EVP is heard.

Specifically, Joanne says, "When my grandfather was alive, he came down here..." At this point, a loud male groan is heard in the background—a very loud groan. And it is clearly an EVP because nobody in the room reacted to the sound at all (something we would obviously do if we heard a male voice make that sound). The groan itself is interesting in that it could either be interpreted as angry (maybe John?) or simply as a response to the word "grandfather."

Could the spirit of the grandfather still be in the trailer—or more accurately—attached to the land in some manner? This was an angle that had not been considered, but made a lot of sense.

Oftentimes spirits seem to want to stick around to atone for the deeds they did while alive—or are so attached to doing worldly things that they don't want to move on. Both of these could be a great excuse for Joanne's relative to still be present on the property. It was just one more detail that had to be considered in the case. Now that I had even more audio evidence to relay to the Martins, it seemed that I would get the chance to discuss the grandfather again with Joanne.

Unfortunately, though, major changes would occur in the Martin household and I would not get the chance to follow up with my findings...

Drastic Changes

Though I had gathered significantly more evidence concerning the haunting of the Martin property, it became abundantly clear that I would not be returning there again—at least not if I wanted to talk with Joanne or her family. Not long after the blessing of the trailer (or the ineffectual blessing, if you want to believe Joanne), the family decided it would be better if they moved out of the cursed abode. This was probably their best decision ever!

Over the years, I have learned that when a family goes through a lot of traumatic, paranormal experiences in a place, it's often impossible to move past them and to live comfortably in that home again. And though it may be the most drastic form of resolution to deal with a haunting, sometimes it's simply a necessary means to an end. If nothing else, moving out would ensure that Julie and Katie would no longer be exposed to something that may potentially scar them psychologically for life.

I asked Patricia and Terri what made Joanne finally decide to leave and they told me an interesting couple of tales…Apparently, the family was staying with relatives and was telling them about the horrible things that had happened to them while living in the trailer. Rather than getting sympathy, or even empathy, the family members thought it was "cool" that there were ghosts in the trailer.

As mentioned previously, one male relative had already decided he would go "ghost busting" at the trailer and ended up getting more than he bargained for. According to Terri, he arrived at the trailer and was checking things out when he heard a loud bang in the living room.

When he walked into that area, his overnight bag flew through the air, striking the wall beside him. He promptly fled into the night with the distinction of being the shortest-lived paranormal investigator ever to enter the field! Apparently, since this incident, even more of the Martin clan (and most likely friends as well) had visited and been frightened away from the property.

Another incident (not long after my visit) was a little more sobering, and it involved Joanne's youngest daughter—Katie Martin. According to Terri, Joanne was cleaning up the trailer when the small girl suddenly began to behave erratically and started crawling all over the floor (she's well beyond the toddler years, so this was not typical behavior). As Joanne questioned her, the girl began taking off her clothes and speaking incoherently. A frantic call was made to Terri, who then dispatched an ambulance to the Martin residence.

Young Katie was kept at the hospital for a week for observation, and Terri would go on to learn from Julie that Joanne was now addicted to crystal methamphetamines and that Katie had gotten into her stash! Yipes…I could still remember hearing Joanne dismiss the drug paraphernalia we found in her trailer as belonging to her tenants.

Katie's incident would go on to be reported to child protective services in Mississippi and the family would end up moving again—this time to be with relatives in

California. I didn't know if this was to avoid having Katie taken away permanently or if they simply wanted to be as far away from the home in Mississippi as possible. Either scenario could have been the case.

As far as the trailer was concerned, Joanne planned to sell it (separate from the family land) so that it could be relocated with a new owner. It would be interesting to know if the paranormal activity goes with it (though I rather doubt it and believe the haunting has more to do with the land and the surrounding area than it does with the trailer itself). But finding a buyer for a trailer in such a dilapidated state would certainly be a challenge.

Luckily, Terri and Patricia were able to meet with Joanne one last time (before she was completely relocated in California) to discuss the final round of evidence we gathered during our final investigation—and to obtain permission from her for me to write this book—before she moved west. She seemed pleased that many of her family's claims had been validated with audio data, but I would not get the chance to discuss the findings with her personally.

Observations and Suggestions

Oftentimes, it's hard to separate a haunting from the family that's experiencing a haunting. In the case of the Martins this is especially true. Would "John," "Keith," "Emily," or possible even a grandfather haunt that trailer if they had not been there? Or even more pertinent, would there have been any activity had they not been the people using instigators (the magic rituals and paraphernalia, the Ouija board, etc.)?

I feel that some stories just have to come out. If a man named John was, indeed, killed by a member of the Martin family—or came to a horrible demise there without their help—it's probable that *something* would have eventually happened to someone there.

Tuning into the paranormal by using occult practices and other mystical means simply helped usher the activity along. Things like Ouija boards are not, in themselves, anything mysterious or magical. (It *is* a board game by Hasbro after all). But when the human mind wills something to happen and there are spirits paying attention, things happen. Things that aren't always explainable or even completely understandable. Such are the circumstances of this case.

In the end, my suggestions to Joanne and her family would have included the possibility of her moving away from the trailer and leaving her family land behind. It is clear from her opinion regarding the blessing of the home that neither she, nor her daughters, would have ever felt completely at ease there. After enduring some of the experiences they related, who would? And with so much negative, possibly nonhuman, activity going on as well, it seemed an even better decision for them to move on.

I'm just glad they decided to do it on their own and that I didn't have to drive back down to them and tell them I thought they should leave!

After all of this, it would be some time before I would hear anything further about the cursed trailer or the Martin family, but it was (of course) inevitable that I would.

9

A Final Trip

After a few months without any word from the Mississippi team or anyone in the Martin family, I was contacted once again out of the blue by Terri. The circumstances concerning my favorite paranormal location in the Mississippi delta had changed again.

Terri informed me that Joanne and her family were once again living in the area—in a home closer to town, though she still owned and was renting out the trailer—and that they were making another attempt to get some answers concerning the haunting of the family land.

To this end, she had invited yet another paranormal group to the site, who intended to perform an investigation the upcoming weekend. Terri wanted to know if I could also be present because things in the trailer had evolved to some strange new territory. She also hoped that my experiences there might serve to assist with the new investigation.

Though this new information sounded a bit cryptic, I was intrigued enough with the case to actually brave the drive back south once again. Plus, I had to admit that I was curious about the current state of the haunting.

However, I knew from past experiences that most paranormal groups do not relish the thought of "outsiders" joining their investigation. So I did not want to interfere with what the new group (we'll call them "X Paranormal" for reference sake) was doing at the trailer at all. Instead, I would simply return to catch up on what had happened with Joanne and her family, take a look at this "new territory" that Terri had referenced, and (perhaps) bring about some sort of resolution concerning the case—at least for myself!

So, after loading considerably less gear than on my previous trips, I found myself once again making the dreaded drive into Mississippi…

A New Approach

Once I arrived at the trailer (already exhausted from the trip), it was immediately obvious that X Paranormal had a whole different approach to an investigation than I did. There were at least fifteen people present to comb through the small trailer, and they seemed to be everywhere, getting into each other's way.

Once I had parked, I looked around and quickly picked out Terri and Tom from the members of the new group. This was no challenge since they were the only ones not dressed in black T-shirts. Sheesh…it looked like an AC/DC concert! Patricia and Blake would not be present for this investigation for personal reasons, but I was certainly glad there were a couple of familiar faces with me at the property. I slowly made my way to them as I watched the new team set up.

As I walked over to introduce myself, it was also quite clear that X Paranormal liked to use a lot of gear. By this I mean huge amounts of gear. In addition to a massive, wired DVR system with multiple cameras stationed all around the trailer (inside and outside), they also had entire tables covered with audio devices, various EMF detectors, and camcorders. It appeared that their approach to an investigation was to bombard an area with as much electronic equipment as is possible.

While on the surface this may seem like a good idea, I have learned the hard way in the past that electronic equipment often interferes with each other—the signals from wireless walkie-talkies pick up the wireless cameras, and so on. As a result, I usually choose to deploy gear more strategically rather than overload a location.

Also, wired DVR systems often make for a cumbersome investigation. Looking at this group's setup, it was clear that people would be tripping over wires all night long. A couple portable camcorders would have most likely served them better since they could be moved rather quickly to areas of activity—and since they are battery powered, they wouldn't trip up any investigator moving through the pitch of night.

But tripping over wires would prove to be the least of my worries for this investigation …

Because there was still no power in the trailer, X Paranormal was running a generator on site to power their massive amounts of gear. A loud generator. A generator that would, most likely, pollute all the audio gathered during the investigation. They had attempted to place the generator as far away from the trailer as possible—but I knew it would still be there, looming in the background of all the audio data collected.

I had hoped to discreetly leave an audio recorder on the premises to gather a few more EVPs during my visit, but after seeing (and hearing) the generator, this idea flew out the window. I would have to be content with updated info and a few new photographs.

After saying my hellos to Terri and Tom, they took me around the area and quickly introduced me to members of the new group. Before they could get indignant at my presence, I quickly explained that my visit was solely for "journalistic purposes," but the leader of the group (I'll call her "Pam") insisted that I still log all my gear into their notebook for tracking purposes. Huh?

I explained that the only "gear" I would be using was my personal camera and that it did not need to be "tracked" since it would remain on my person during my visit, but this was like arguing with a wall—an illogical wall. She insisted that this was just their practice. So, rather than debating the ridiculousness of me logging *my* gear in *their* notebook (and adding on to the sizable amount of gear that they were already tracking during their visit), I simply placated them and left shaking my head. But the ridiculousness was not over.

Terri then explained to me that Pam wanted to bring all the investigators over to do a "blessing" before they did any work in the trailer. I probably don't have to tell you that I was appalled by this idea. Blessing? What kind of blessing? What possible benefit would this provide concerning the performance of a scientific investigation of the paranormal at this location? The short answer: none.

It was clear that this was *not* going to be a scientific investigation. Not long after the prayer circle broke up, I could hear Pam lecturing her team members about wearing anything religious that could "provoke" the demonic entity in the trailer into doing anything to them. Wow. If wearing a cross or crucifix antagonized anything in the trailer, wouldn't doing a blessing in the front yard essentially make them all targets? It made no sense.

Without ever having investigated the location, X Paranormal had already come to the hasty conclusion that they were dealing with a demonic presence. I was sure this pleased Joanne. Finally, some paranormal types were actually humoring her and giving her the attention that she desired.

I pulled Terri to the side and asked her about this. I could not believe that she and Tom were actually interested in being a part of such a debacle. At this point, Terri filled me in on some new events that had happened at the trailer during my absence.

The Haunted Meth Lab

Apparently, not long after returning to Mississippi, Joanne decided, once again, to try to rent the trailer. However, this time the tenants would get the entire place, since Joanne had no intention in living there herself. And despite missing two windows and being trashed, she managed to actually get a couple interested in living there—and it wasn't long before they moved in. For anyone other than Joanne, this would have set off alarms. Who would live in such conditions? The short answer: meth addicts.

Not long after the tenants had moved into the trailer, Joanne stopped getting her reasonably low amount of rent money from the couple. Concerned, she visited the property several times to try and collect the payments—to no avail. Either she never found them at home, or they were hiding in the trailer when she went over. Eventually, she was forced to go through legal channels to have the tenants evicted from the trailer.

Once they were gone, Joanne visited the trailer and found that it was (somehow) in an even worse state than before. But worse than that, it was clear that the people had been making crystal meth inside the premises. A quick look around the place found drug paraphernalia, all the ingredients necessary for concocting the drug, and the scent of the recently cooked amphetamines still hung heavy in the air.

There also happened to be something else in the trailer—something that Joanne, even with her basic occult background, did not immediately recognize as being of significance.

In the kitchen of the trailer, a large mound of dirt was heaped up on the dining room table with assorted items strewn about it. According to the investigators of X Paranormal, this mound of dirt, along with the various items present, held specific occult significance. Basically, they were the essential ingredients needed for summoning the Devil or a demon through the use of a magic ritual.

The dirt was assumed by the group to be "grave dirt," and several items that were present held a specific purpose for this ritual—or so X Paranormal believed. These items included a pack of juniper berries and a small silver bell that I was told the entity is supposed to ring upon its arrival to let the summoner know it is present.

After Terri finished explaining all of this, she took me inside the trailer to show me the pile of dirt in the kitchen, along with the various occult items. Knowing nothing about magical rituals, I would just have to take the word of X Paranormal that this was what was going on in the trailer: meth heads summoning the Devil! But Terri had even more information for me—news that made the latest deeds of the trailer seem even more sinister.

According to Terri, not long after the tenants were evicted, they were involved in a deadly accident that claimed the life of the female resident. This was told to me with bated breath and a tremor in her voice. She believed it was a result of the couple meddling with the occult.

While there could be no way to possibly know this to be the case, I did not press the issue with Terri or X

Paranormal. After all, I have my own weird tale that involves the Devil, and I certainly did not want to challenge their personal beliefs. Nonetheless, I did have Terri escort me through the trailer, so that I could photograph the table with the dirt and items, as well as to see the damage the couple had wrought upon the place.

As we walked through the premises, I snapped my photos and held my nose tightly—believe it or not, the heavy scent of the cooked drugs was still in the air! Members of X Paranormal moved around us, quickly opening windows to air out the trailer for their investigation (a move that was needed, but would further pollute their audio data with the sounds outside the home).

Once we were finished with the walkthrough, Terri then informed me that X Paranormal had made another discovery on the property as well: the location of John's grave!

The Mysterious Mound

After I was finished taking all the photos that I needed, Terri and I made our way back outside. Fighting our way past cables running from the DVR system into the house, Terri then took me around to the back of the trailer to an area that featured a deep depression with a large mound in the center of it. This, according to all present, was the gravesite of John.

I took a slow walk around the depression, taking photos all the while. There was no way for me to know if what they were saying was true. If there had been a John and he had been killed on the property in the 1940s, he would have most likely been placed in the ground quite a long time ago. There would be no evidence on the surface of the ground to indicate if there was a body there.

So I asked Terri how they knew he was buried there and if they had tried to dig for bones or other physical evidence. She told me that nobody had done any digging, but that the X Paranormal team had confirmed the gravesite through the use of dowsing rods. What?! I immediately stopped taking photos and left the area. I had a hard time believing that Terri, or Tom for that matter, could possibly believe that they had found a grave by using dowsing rods! Clearly the X Paranormal group was rubbing off on them.

In the paranormal world, though, there are many different beliefs—and the use of many different investigation methods. To those on the outside, the use of dowsing rods or a psychic may be no more ridiculous an investigative method than running audio and video recorders. After all, ghosts are make-believe, right?

But for those of us on the inside, there is a definite dividing line between those who stick to a strictly scientific method (like myself) and those who use techniques like pendulums, crystals, psychics, dowsing rods…well, you get the picture.

As a result, I knew it would do no good to scoff at their claims that there was a grave behind the trailer. That would just spawn a heated debate about the paranormal and various techniques. I told Terri to let me know if they ever got any *proof* that a person was buried in the mound. As of the writing of this book, this has not happened—and I don't really expect that it will…

Terri would, however, send me the link to an article from a local news source that detailed the death of the tenant who had passed away in the accident, so that was an actual incident.

A Final Investigation

Though I had no intention of joining in on X Paranormal's investigation, I stuck around while they did it. It went pretty much like how any other group would do such a thing: equipment was stationed throughout the trailer, members took turns making their rounds through the place, and on occasion, somebody would claim to have seen or heard something. Most of these incidents were of the mundane nature, but they did break up the monotony.

At one point, several audio recorders were reviewed on the spot, with one member claiming to have gotten a set of strange EVPs that he claimed was made by a "Native American" voice. I listened to one of the EVPs and could not hear what the investigator was talking about.

Even though their team did a reasonably good job of maintaining noise discipline, they were still working in a small trailer with the windows open, people talking outside, and a generator running in the vicinity!

So of course the audio recorder had caught something—most likely random noise—though I had no idea where the whole Native American thing came from…Thus far, nobody had ever mentioned any possibility of a Native American spirit being present. But, hey, Joanne believed in everything, right?

After observing for a couple hours, I decided to make another pass with my infrared camera to take some additional photos, and then I said my goodbyes. I had learned a lot from my final trip to the trailer: I learned that it was destined to stay knee-deep in illegal drugs, that people seemed to like doing occult and magic-oriented activities in the place, and that word that the place is haunted was beginning to make its rounds through the local paranormal community.

I was also sure that Joanne was most likely pleased with all of this. After all, it was most likely attention that she had wanted in the first place—whether it was from the living or the dead.

The Aftermath

So, after two full-length investigations, a third visit to the trailer, and over a hundred hours spent reviewing evidence from this case, what did I learn?

First off, I learned that the word "haunting" is a broad term and that it should only serve as a jumping off point for investigating the paranormal. Trying to set hard definitions on what a "poltergeist" or "demonic infestation" means is simply setting yourself up for failure. It's important to go in to a case with an open mind and to simply observe and record the happenings that are occurring there. In the end, only the evidence matters—not what label you attach to the activity.

I also learned that "evil" and "demonic" are subjective terms. They can mean completely different things to different people. A Catholic and a Baptist have completely different ideas about how the Devil works—and if there are even demons capable of intruding upon the lives of the living. And religions other than Christianity have their own beliefs concerning these phenomena as well. So it's best to avoid using these terms—or to venture into the realm of the religious at all.

In the end, only one set of beliefs is important when we are investigating the paranormal: the beliefs of the client. Ultimately, they are the ones who have to live within the haunted environment and have to feel comfortable in their own home. It is not our place as investigators to push our beliefs upon them.

Unfortunately, Joanne seemed to have no real belief system other than believing there were several spirits in her home. And without having any way to comfort her in this regard, it made working on her case an almost impossible task. Joanne didn't want to be comforted, and she didn't believe that house blessings had any effect. She also didn't want to live free of fear, despite saying that she did.

What she wanted was someone to tell her she was right and that something horrible was there in her trailer—along with her ex-husband in tow. Short of that, paranormal investigators were really of no use to her. Though she did not feel comfortable with living in the trailer, it was clear that she didn't mind it being haunted. After all, it was supplying her with attention and company.

Which brings me to perhaps the most important lesson I learned from this case: clients want a resolution, but it's not always the resolution that we think. It's not always enough to visit a client's home, set up and use a bunch of gear, and then play them some audio/video clips. They want to know, "What do you plan to do about all this?"

If a paranormal investigator isn't prepared to offer some sort of resolution for a client, then he or she may be better off sticking to haunted hotels, restaurants, and museums for their ghostly fill.

For this particular case, and the Martin family, resolution was a particular sticky wicket—though I think, in the end, Joanne sort of got the resolution she wanted: validation that something paranormal was happening in her home, whether she and her family created the situation or not.

For most families, this is not the resolution they are looking for!

Bringing Resolution

When it comes to the well-being of a family and helping them to feel psychologically sound within their own environment, resolution usually means directly addressing the issue of spirits being present.

While recording the testimony of what's happening within a haunted location, it's best to pay attention to the way the details of the haunting are being told. Is the client using a lot of religious or occult terms? Are they exhibiting any fear or are they excited by the prospect of a ghost? Not everyone is frightened of paranormal activity. How do they feel about the haunting?

Paying attention to the attitude of the client is the key to bringing resolution to a haunting. If they are afraid, you must assuage this fear. This could mean a simple blessing (one that anyone can perform), a religious blessing (by clergy), or even helping the residents to directly confront the entity on their property and to ask them to leave.

It's surprising how many times doing these things has had a positive impact on a client—especially if they are experiencing an intelligent spirit. And all of this is much better than telling a client that they will have to leave their home for any kind of solution to their problem.

Another thing worth noting is the issue of dealing with children. First off, don't say anything to a child without telling the parent what you're going to say. Again, you don't want to confuse the child by giving them information that conflicts with household beliefs. Second, the best way to explain anything concerning a ghost to child is to simply relate to them that the spirit was once a person just like them and that they may simply be lonely or lost.

It's also important to not place any malicious intent where there is none; if something of an infernal nature is taking place, the parents will most likely remove their children from the home until there is a resolution. Nothing should be done beyond this. Causing any psychological damage to a child (or anyone else for that matter), even accidentally, can make a permanent impact on them and should be avoided at all costs. In other words, don't scare the hell out of them!

The Martin case also solidified my belief that psychics should be avoided when investigating the paranormal. Imagine what would have happened to me on this case if I had taken along a "psychic" who sputtered out incredible information to the Martin family in order to support their claims. Things could have gotten out of hand in a hurry.

Every psychic I have ever met has spat out useless, unsupportable guesses or information I already had gotten from a quick Google search. Fraudulent psychics simply want attention and want to feel special. And until we are able to tell the real deal from the fake, they must be put aside.

Understanding hauntings, ghosts, and other areas of the paranormal means researching and investigating these phenomena using scientific methods and techniques. Understanding a *particular* haunting means listening carefully to the client and respecting their wishes and beliefs. When we do these two things, we all find resolution.

Well…the client gets resolution. We, as investigators, often get none. We are, more often than not, still as confused about a case leaving it as we were when we found it. But this is reasonable, right?

After all, we are investigating the paranormal…

Epilogue

As I mentioned in the introduction, this book was never intended to be specifically about the Martin case in Mississippi. I wanted to present a realistic picture of what perspective investigators might encounter while working in the field on private cases.

It would have been easy to dramatize the Martin case and to write a book much like those I read in my youth: scary! But while doing that may have made for an entertaining read, it would have been a grave disservice to everyone who wants to know what it's really like to investigate a haunting.

Now that you have read *Devil in the Delta*, I encourage you to visit the website of my group, Paranormal Inc (www .paranormalincorporated.com). In the right sidebar of the website is a list of many of the investigations we have done over the years—just click on one you want to check out and you can read case details, listen to EVPs captured during our investigation, and sometimes even see photographs and videos from the case.

Many of the cases mentioned in this book (such as those detailed in chapter 4) are on the website, so you can actually check out some of the evidence mentioned here in this book. In addition to this, I have added a link for the Martin case. If you go to that particular link, you will get to see more photographs taken at the location, hear the audio files I reference in this book, and get even more details about the case and my investigation there.

I hope this book serves as a friendly warning to everyone who is contemplating investigating the paranormal—but I also hope it does not scare you off completely from the venture! As I have written in this book, as well as the other books I have written for Llewellyn Publishing, there are lots of great haunted locations open to the public that you can visit and enjoy. Possibly even investigate. So have fun and let me know how your investigations go. Cheers!

If you think you've caught the ghost hunting bug, here's an excerpt from *Ghost Hunting for Beginners*.

Pre-Investigation:

Getting Started

Preparing for an investigation can be a daunting task. Besides making arrangements and getting your gear together, you will also have to mentally prepare for the possibility of encountering the paranormal. Of course, this is exactly what we, as investigators, want. Many believe it's sort of politically incorrect to admit the desire to meet up with a ghost, but the truth is that nobody would go into this field without wanting to find one!

That said, preparing for a night at a haunted location begins as soon as you have gotten your case. Right now, let's just say you've gotten the case and now it's your mission to conduct a professional and thorough investigation. It should be mentioned at this point that ANY case you take on should be done WITH PERMISSION. Every place is owned by someone—and that person should give you permission to investigate on their property. But, hey, you're going to be a responsible investigator, right? So you will have permission.

It's best to approach a new haunted location in three stages: Pre-Investigation, Investigation, and Post-Investigation.

Pre-Investigation

The first and foremost thought in your mind as a new investigator should be, "How do I approach this case *professionally?*" In most fields, certain methodologies and techniques lend more to an individual being taken seriously than a certain attitude does. In the realm of the paranormal, though, it has everything to do with approach and results. Now, some of you reading this will ask, "Isn't that the same thing?" Nope. Let me explain…

In a field where everything is under scrutiny and hotly debated, all methodologies are given equal keel. Scientific groups get just as much business as those that prefer to utilize psychics. It's a matter of personal taste as to who an individual will contact for assistance. So, chances are, whatever method you prefer for an investigation, there will be people out there who agree with you. But one thing that all potential clients want is a professional approach.

Being Professional

Being professional means actually preparing in advance for an investigation rather than just showing up with some gear and buddies. It means concentrating on gathering evidence vs. giggling/laughing and cutting up with your group members. And it also means assuaging the concerns and fears of the property owners to bring about a resolution to their case. Though it's almost impossible to prepare in advance for the excitement (or fear) involved with an actual encounter, every other item I just mentioned can be managed. And it all starts with how you treat the client.

Though it should be a no-brainer, the obvious must be stated here: respect your clients and their locations! If you say you're going to be at their home at 5 p.m., then be there! If they tell you not to touch their antique collection of beer cans, then keep your paws off of them! For people to feel comfortable with strangers roaming about their home or business there has to be a measure of trust—and this can be easily lost, so tread carefully. Though you may not think so, another basic step to being professional is *looking* professional.

Think about it from the client's perspective: Let's say you have been experiencing scary voices and objects moving in your house. And you have a small child as well. You don't know what's happening and you're afraid for your family so you call your local paranormal group. Then they show up unkempt, unorganized, and they're all wearing black T-shirts emblazoned with a ghost that's straight out of a horror movie. How much confidence would you have in this organization?

This is an important consideration even if you plan to investigate a park, abandoned building, or cemetery because—somebody always owns the property. Whether it's the city, the county, or a private entity, ALL locations are governed by someone and you must get permission and respect their wishes.

One last suggestion I have concerning respect is this: if you inform a client exactly what you plan to do, you will be able to do more! Many times over the years I have visited a haunted hotel and been amazed by what they will allow me to do when I tell them what I want to do and ask them for permission. These are the cases that, when I post them in a book or on our website, other paranormal groups send me emails saying, "How did you get into that place? Nobody's ever gotten to investigate there!" I asked. That's how.

Now that you have resolved to be a professional investigator, let's talk about what should be the first step to every investigation: research.

Research Strategies
Of all the things that separate serious paranormal investigators from thrill-seekers, research is probably the greatest. For people who simply want to be "scared" and to "see a ghost," spending hours in a local library going through old newspaper records is the least appealing trip possible. For

those of us that want answers, though, this is often the first step to any investigation.

Though the Internet can often be the first step in your research process, it can't be the *entire* process. Some Internet sources pride themselves on getting the facts straight concerning the history and paranormal activity of a location, but the vast majority of them will accept their "facts" from any source with no verification whatsoever. This makes for a lousy investigation and often just perpetuates urban legends.

Often the best Internet source for a location is that specific location's website (if they have one). Many bed and breakfasts, hotels, restaurants, etc., list their own history right on their sites. Some even include ghost stories and sightings (with the popularity of the paranormal on the rise, many have found marketing their haunting to be a good thing). But, again, this should only be your first stop. Getting out of the house and going to local sources will get you far more useful information.

The local library, historical societies, newspapers, and city hall are great sources of information. Since visiting even one of these places may mean hours of work, you should allow for a at least day of research prior to a night of investigation). Your first stop should be the library.

In addition to archiving local newspaper articles, librarians are skilled at pulling historical documents and often know a lot about local history. They may point you to sources that aren't listed anywhere (such as people in the community who may remember a specific event or an author who wrote about a certain place). I've discovered that a portable flatbed scanner is often invaluable during these trips as you can digitally archive everything you need and save money by not making copies at the library. Once you have all the info you can get at the library, you may consider some of the other mentioned stops.

If a newspaper was around during the heyday of the site you're investigating, they may have some useful articles in their archives. Historical societies are usually run by historians who specialize in local history and often have an amazing amount of knowledge about any given house, hotel, or local property. And a town's city hall will have information regarding property transactions (great for seeing who owned a place during a specific time), birth and death records, and even marriage licenses. These sources will help you fill in any gaps that you may have about the history of a family or property.

Often, as you learn more about a specific event, location, or person, you will slowly begin to understand just how much of a ghost story is actually urban legend. Separating the myth from fact is one of the best things you can do prior to your investigation, as it will save you time investigating the wrong thing! For example, local legend may state that "Aunt Martha" haunts the old Miller place. If you discover that Aunt Martha doesn't exist, you can avoid hours of EVP work asking Martha questions.

Conversely, just because you have the complete history of a family and their property, it shouldn't affect your investigation to the point that you have tunnel vision. Let's say a property has always been in the Miller family; it would be easy to assume that a member of the Miller family haunts the house. But what if there was a previous house at that site? Or maybe there was a significant battle when the area was a grassy hill. The history of any location is a long one—and you can bet we only know a small percentage of it.

Lastly, I want to touch on a different type of research—one that's more about the logistics of performing your investigation. This is usually done directly with the residents of a place. Before prepping for your visit, you will want to know if a place has power and if they have any activity outside, in which case weather may be a factor and you will have to rely on battery power. This will also affect your clothing, gear, etc. Knowing all this will help you have a successful investigation.

Equipment Maintenance

It's amazing how often this step is overlooked by even seasoned investigators—myself included. Current technology dictates that much of the gear that we use (especially digital cameras, camcorders, and audio recorders) has to be charged up before use. Whether you make it one of the last steps you do after an investigation (plugging in your gear for a fresh charge can be done during your review of the data you've collected) or one of the first before heading out, make sure that all of your gear—as well as any additional chargeable batteries—are all good to go.

Of course there's also plenty of equipment that operates on good ole store-bought, single-use batteries, so stock up on the sizes that your team uses (usually AA, AAA, and 9 volt). There's a running joke in the paranormal community that batteries are "ghost bait" due to the fact that many devices/batteries end up inexplicably drained during an investigation. I have found this to be completely true, so don't just take enough batteries to fill your equipment—take enough so that you can power up all your gear several times. There's nothing worse than having some great activity going on all around you and suddenly having no batteries to put in your audio recorder to capture it all.

In addition to making sure your gear has power, you will also want to perform common-sense maintenance. This means cleaning off the lenses on your cameras ("orbs" captured at haunted locations are often nothing more than dust on the lens) and dusting off and cleaning gear that's stationed outside.

When you dress for an investigation, dress logically! Besides wearing comfortable clothes, make sure you wear items that will easily identify you to other team members and passersby. If you're all dressed in black and you're walking around in the background of a camera, it's easy to mistake you for a "shadow mass" or entity. Don't worry about looking cool and dressing all in black. Worry about being safe and conducting a good investigation.

Choosing Your Team

Deciding who to take along with you on your ghost adventures may be one of the most important decisions you make. Besides the fact that you want individuals with the same paranormal belief system (What use is a psychic on your team if nobody else believes in psychics?), you will want to take along people that you trust implicitly. If a member of your team approaches you with an eyewitness account of a full-bodied apparition, there should be no doubt that what he or she is saying is true.

Because most people only have a handful of friends they trust in this capacity, many paranormal groups opt to keep their team small. My group, Paranormal Inc, has only three members—and the other two are my brother and a friend I have known for over twenty years! Another advantage to having a small group is the lower likelihood of contaminating your own audio/video footage. The fewer folk that you have tramping around a house, the less people you have to worry about keeping track of. Ideally, you should know where everyone is at all times by tagging your audio/video (more on this later) and keeping a log book during your investigation, but when you have a large number of people, doing this is almost impossible.

Unfortunately, many paranormal groups go to extreme lengths to get as many "members" as they can. They do membership drives, constantly recruit, and often do open investigations that allow untrained individuals to wander throughout the location. What's the point of this? Evidence gathered during such an investigation cannot be taken seriously due to the high probability of contamination. If you are looking for a social club (and there's nothing wrong with making ghost hunting a social activity) then make your group a social club!

When you make your decisions concerning your team, consider making it as diverse as possible, too. Try to have at least one female member and one male member. Experience has taught me that some entities have an easier time responding to a certain gender than another.

Of course, many paranormal enthusiasts go another route. Since some people do not have any friends interested in the paranormal and don't want to join an existing group, many opt for investigating by themselves. This is perfectly acceptable, within reason. If you are going to a place with on-site workers and patrons (such as a hotel, B&B, restaurant), you should have no problem investigating on your own. Just watch your step while moving around in the dark and keep your cell phone in your pocket (though turned off so it doesn't interfere with your equipment).

I certainly do not advise doing an investigation at an outdoor location by yourself—there are simply too many factors beyond your control (wild animals, weather, terrain, etc.). There is also a practical reason to have at least one other investigator with you—if you see/hear a paranormal event, it's nice to have that corroborating witness!

Interviews

One of the most important things you can do when you arrive at a haunted location is to conduct interviews with the clients/inhabitants. Some choose to do this by phone or email prior to visiting, but for most this is a logical first step when you arrive at the actual haunted place. To this end, try to interview everyone who has experienced anything out of the ordinary—and, if possible, record your interviews using an audio recorder. (Be courteous and ask permission first!) And as you interview them, you will want to concentrate on a few different talking points.

First, make sure to get as much information as you can concerning the specific paranormal events. Where and when did they happen? What was the duration of the event? And so on. With enough information, you may be able to identify patterns concerning the activity, which, in turn, will direct you to the locations that have the highest probability of turning up evidence for you to capture. Other key questions to also ask include:

1. How would you describe the paranormal events you are experiencing?

2. Are you frightened by the events that are taking place?

3. Have you noticed any strange, but seemingly natural, problems recently? (Electrical, plumbing, etc.)

4. Do you believe in ghosts? Are you active in any church/religion?

5. What is the history of the location? (Concentrate on any traumatic events or deaths that may have taken place at the site.)

6. Are you currently taking any drugs, prescription or otherwise?

7. Have there been any recent traumatic events in the home?

This line of questioning should give you enough background information to determine what, exactly, is going on, what has happened there in the past, and where you can expect something to occur during your visit. After you have finished up your interviews, you will then want to perform a walkthrough of the location.

Walkthrough

Besides giving you the layout of the property, the walkthrough will also provide you with the technical information you need to conduct a good investigation. You also will be surprised how many more memories are jogged when you're actually walking through a place; some people experience a lot at certain haunted sites so it makes sense that they may not be able to remember all of it while sitting at the kitchen table for an interview!

As you perform your walkthrough, make a rudimentary map of the location and make notes of special areas. There are four types of areas you will want to note:

1. Hot spots. These are specific locations where something of a paranormal nature has taken place. Whether it's disembodied voices, a person that was touched, or even an apparition, you will want to particularly pay attention to these areas. As you mark these places on your map, you may want to assign an appropriate piece of equipment. (i.e., if the owner has often heard moans in the living room, consider placing an audio recorder there)

2. Off limits areas. These are locations that the owners/clients do not want you to intrude upon. Respect their wishes! There are usually have good reasons. If you go to a lot of hotels, restaurants, etc., you will encounter these spots quite often.

3. Trouble areas. These are places that may pose a unique challenge to your investigation. Examples of these are places where it may be dangerous to be at night (sharp corners, big steps, etc.), are close to an air conditioning unit (the noise may pollute your audio), or are even extremely bright because of outside light sources you cannot control (the use of some infrared equipment may be inadvisable).

4. Power sources. Since battery drainage is always a problem at investigations—sometimes because of paranormal interference, sometimes because they just went dead—it's always good to mark working power outlets. A lot of gear can be plugged into an electrical socket, and this should be taken advantage of whenever possible.

Besides logistics, the walkthrough can help you determine what is normal for the site. While you are making your way around the location and making notes on your map with the owner/client, you should have your other team members follow behind you to take base readings. Noting the average temperature and EMF (electromagnetic field) reading for each room will help you during the night to determine whether an encounter is natural or of a possible paranormal nature. This is also a great opportunity to inform the client of your intentions while you investigate. The more information they have concerning your methodologies, etc., the more at ease they will feel about having strangers there on their property.

You also can take some reference photos of each area as well; when you are back at home and performing a review of your evidence, it's sometimes helpful to be able to "see" the room once again. For instance, if you come across a photograph that seems to have a dark figure standing in a corner, you can go back to your reference photos to see if that entity was actually just a floor lamp!

Many of these pre-investigation techniques require nothing more than curiousity and careful observeration—tools that someone with even a casual interest in the paranormal can make use of during a public tour of a haunted location.

Learning the nuts and bolts of how to conduct an actual investigation and review the data collected is too detailed to cover in an excerpt. However, these tips should get you started thinking like a ghost hunter.